A Study of...

GOD'S
HEBREW
NAMES

MICHAEL L. GOWENS

Sovereign Grace Publications
Shallotte, North Carolina

A STUDY OF GOD'S HEBREW NAMES
Published by Sovereign Grace Publications, LLC
Post Office Box 1150
Shallotte, North Carolina 28459
www.sovgrace.net
sovgracepublications@gmail.com

ISBN 978-1-929635-26-9

Printed in the United States of America.

CONTENTS

Introduction
God's Name Revealed

"I have manifested thy name unto the men that thou gavest me out of the world."
John 17:6a

R evelation is a humbling doctrine. It is humbling because it assumes the premise that man never would have known God by himself (cf. Job 11:7-9; Mt. 11:25-27; 16:17; Jno. 1:18; 1 Cor. 2:9-12; 1 Tim. 6:15-16). The infinite God is ultimately incomprehensible[1]—that is, there is more to his essential Being than finite minds can ever fully grasp (Job 5:9; 26:14; 37:23; Ps. 77:19; 145:3; Ecc. 3:11; Rom. 11:33)—and the minds of fallen sinners are fundamentally fallen and depraved (Gen. 6:5; Rom. 8:7; 1 Cor. 2:14; Eph. 4:18), making it impossible to discover God on our own. Had God not been pleased to reveal himself to humanity, we would all be worshiping at the altar of "the unknown God" (Acts 17:23).

But there is good news. God has been pleased to graciously disclose himself to man. He has revealed himself both generally, in the universe he made (cf. Ps. 8:1-9; Ps. 19:1-1-6), and specially, in Holy Scripture (Ps. 19:7-11; Rom. 16:25-26). In terms of special revelation, God has made himself known, first, by disclosing his various names; secondly, by the record of his actions in history (Rom. 1:18; 9:17); and thirdly, by sending his own Son into the world (Jno. 1:14,18; Col. 1:19; 2:9; Heb. 1:3). We may know what God is like by these various means, not the least of which are the names, together with the particular nuance intrinsic to each one, revealed in the pages of God's revealed word.

---

[1] When theologians say that God is "incomprehensible," they do not mean that man is unable to know *anything* about God, but rather that man is unable to know *everything* about God.

When the Lord Jesus prayed "*I have manifested thy name unto the men that thou gavest me out of the world.*" (Jno. 17:6a), he did not mean that he had simply divulged a label the disciples might employ when referring to God, but rather that he revealed the Father's character to them. God's name stands for his person: "*Through thee will we push down our enemies: through thy name will we tread them under that rise up against us*" (Ps. 44:8); "*Our help is in the name of the LORD* [Jehovah], *who made heaven and earth*" (Ps. 124:8). That our God has a name indicates that he is a personal God, not some abstract Philosophical X or unquantifiable, amorphous idea, like cosmic dust. No, he has a name: "*Sing unto God* [Elohim], *sing praises to his name: extol him that rideth upon the heavens by his name JAH, and rejoice before him*" (Ps. 68:4).

Show Me Thy Glory

Revelation is also a distinctive doctrine. It distinguishes Judaism, and later Christianity, from the mystery religions (such as Buddhism, Hinduism, Taoism, Confucianism, Shintoism, etc.) which teach that "god" is ultimately unknowable. Though the Lord, indeed, dwells "in thick darkness" (1 Kings 8:12; Ps. 18:11) in terms of the fact that he may not be discovered or known by human investigation, i.e. the natural man will never know God apart from grace (cf. Job 11:7-9) and in that sense, God is shrouded in mystery, yet he has taken the initiative to make himself and his counsels known (Rom. 16:25-26; Eph. 1:9; 3:9-10; Col. 1:26-27; Ps. 98:2). The thick darkness of mystery, in other words, has dissipated in the brightness of God's revealed glory.

Glory might be defined as "God in self-display" or "God shining forth." It suggests the idea of something bright, effulgent, brilliant, clear and open to view. *Glory* is a composite attribute of God—an umbrella concept, if you please—containing all the rest. It speaks of God in comprehensive, superlative terms. When Moses then, encouraged by his previous encounters with God at the burning bush and the Red Sea, as well as the Lord's promise to go before him (cf. Ex. 3, 14, 33:14), dared to ask God for even a further and more complete revelation of the character of God, he defined his request in terms of God's glory: "*I beseech thee, show me thy glory*" (Ex. 33:18).

This request for the beatific vision[2] expresses the deepest yearning of a regenerate heart, i.e. the desire to see the face of God. To ask for a view of the glory of God is to seek to know God without a filter, in all his brilliant majesty and beauty.

The Lord's response to this daring request is supremely instructive to our present study. He answered Moses' prayer with both a denial and an affirmation of the request. The denial is in verse 20: "*And he said, Thou canst not see my face: for there shall no man see me, and live.*" The beatific vision must wait until final glorification (cf. Jno. 1:18a; 1 Tim. 1:17; 6:16; Phi. 3:21; Jno. 17:24; 1 Cor. 13:12; 1 Jno. 3:2). Yet, in another sense, God granted Moses' request: "*And he said, I will make all my goodness pass before thee, and I will proclaim the name of the LORD* (Jehovah) *before thee...and it shall come to pass, while my glory passeth by, that I will put thee in a clift of the rock, and will cover thee with my hand while I pass by: and I will take away mine hand, and thou shalt see my back parts: but my face shall not be seen*" (vs. 19a, 22-23).

Three thoughts are especially significant here. First, notice that in our present state, **the glory of God is largely comprehended in his goodness**, i.e. his sovereign grace and mercy: "*I will make all my goodness pass before thee...and will be gracious to whom I will be gracious, and will show mercy on whom I will show mercy*" (Ex. 33:19b). Although the concept of

---

[2] The "beatific vision" is a popular theological expression, likely coined by Dante in his *Divine Comedy*, to speak of the ultimate, face-to-face, unmediated, direct and complete view of God's glory in heaven. Now we see Him by faith, only partially. But then, we will behold the Lord immediately, viewing His beauty with unmitigated joy and delight. This will be perfect happiness and satisfaction, for there will be nothing left to desire or seek once a person sees the face of God.

glory (Heb. *kabod*) includes the incommunicable attributes of eternality, majesty, immutability, omniscience and omnipotence, we may not fully comprehend these qualities of the infinite God with finite minds, for mortals have no reference point in experience with which to interpret immortality. But we may comprehend in our experience his goodness, for we know our own frailty, weakness and sinfulness. In our present state, the paramount display of God's character is his patience, lovingkindness and tender condescension to favor unworthy men with his blessing. Nothing is more glorious than his amazing grace to sinners. Notice of the nine particular characteristics highlighted in the next chapter's verbal description of God's character (Ex. 34:6-7), seven of them have to do with what we might call his "goodness."

Secondly, this episode teaches that presently, ***the glory of God is primarily heard, not seen***. It is a verbal (not visual) revelation, viewed by faith, i.e. by means of hearing God's word: "*I will proclaim the name of the LORD before thee*" (Ex. 33:19a). Prior to glorification, we may only see the glory of God in the proclamation of his name—that is, his self-revelation in Scripture. Exodus 34:6 captures the scene in this case: "*And the LORD passed by before him, and proclaimed, The LORD* [Jehovah], *The LORD God* [Jehovah Elohim], *merciful and gracious, longsuffering, and abundant in goodness and truth, keeping mercy for thousands, forgiving iniquity and transgression and sin, and that will by no means clear the guilty...*" Even today, we walk by faith, not sight. Until we see him with glorified eyes in heavenly peace, we must see with our ears, forming our conceptions of God by means of special revelation in the word.

Thirdly, notice from this scene that any ***personal experience of the glory of God prior to the eternal state is only partial at best***. Moses saw not God's glorious face, but his "back parts" (Ex. 33:23), i.e. the after-glow, or trailing glory. Like the crowd at a wedding sees the bride's train while her face is veiled, so

Moses saw the residual glory after God passed by. Of course, that sight was glorious enough to make his face shine with such reflective divine beauty that the children of Israel could not sustain an unveiled gaze at him, but still, it was merely a partial and fleeting glance of God. Likewise, our knowledge of God, even though it is indeed the most brilliant spectacle a person may ever behold in this world, is partial and limited at best. But if the gospel message that portrays the blessed Savior of sinners to the eye of faith is so glorious, what a prospect awaits us when we see him face to face?

> *If such the views which grace unfold, weak as it is below,*
> *What rapture shall the Church above in Jesus' presence know!*

Until then, we may be thankful that God has taken the initiative to make himself known by means of his glorious name. He delights to be known, as the very idea of "revelation" suggests, and those who are privileged to view, even partially, his glory will be increasingly transformed by that gaze until they, Moses-like, reflect the brilliance in their own lives. It is with such an end in view that we embark on this study of the several Hebrew names of God revealed in his word.

Hallowing His Holy Name

Revelation is also a very sobering doctrine. It is a great responsibility to be entrusted with the task of safeguarding a precious treasure, and there is no treasure as precious as God's own holy reputation. In fact, it is such a serious responsibility that God includes a Divine prohibition against the irreverent and glib treatment of his name in the Ten Commandments: *"Thou shalt not take the name of the Lord thy God in vain"* (Ex. 20: 7a). Of all the many sins that might have been included, the sin of blasphemy is one of the top ten potential violations of God's moral law.

Psalm 111:9 states that the name of our covenant-keeping,

redeemer God is "holy and reverend." If it is holy, then it should be hallowed. If it is reverend, it should be treated with respect. In the first petition of the Model Prayer, Jesus teaches his disciples to make the sanctifying of God's name the first priority of their daily prayers (cf. Mt. 6:9b). *"Hallowed be thy name"* means "may thy name be regarded as holy." That which is holy is set apart, or distinguished, from everything else. Superior value is assigned to it in contrast to the common, profane and ordinary. When a person prays "Hallowed be thy name," he aligns himself with the Lord's own self-concern for the glory of his own name, ascribing honor and reverential respect to God alone.

Consider the Lord's interest in the glory of his name, as expressed in the promise to restore the exiles in Babylon to their homeland: *"But I had pity for mine holy name, which the house of Israel had profaned among the heathen...Thus saith the Lord GOD* [Adonai Jehovah]; *I do not this for your sakes, O house of Israel, but for mine holy name's sake, which ye have profaned among the heathen, whither ye went. And I will sanctify my great name, which was profaned among the heathen, which ye have profaned in the midst of them; and the heathen shall know that I am the LORD* [Jehovah], *saith the Lord GOD* [Adonai Jehovah], *when I shall be sanctified in you before their eyes. For I will take you from among the heathen, and gather you out of all countries, and will bring you into your own land"* (Eze. 36:21-24).

God's motive in delivering them, in other words, was the hallowing of his own name, not because the people deserved or merited such a kindness. God does all things with a supreme self-regard to the glory of his own name (cf. Is. 42:8; 48:9). If the Lord so highly regards his name, shouldn't we also?

Yet how frequently the name of God is maligned, defamed, and blasphemed by mortal men! As previously noted, the third of the Ten Commandments is a prohibition against blasphemy: *"Thou shalt not take the name of the LORD* [Jehovah] *thy God* [Elohim] *in vain; for the LORD* [Jehovah] *will not hold him guiltless that taketh his name in vain"* (Ex. 20:7). In what way may a person violate this prohibition against blasphemy? First of all, any cavalier, flippant or irreverent use of God's name constitutes the sin of blasphemy, for it fails to ascribe the glory he is due. Because God's name is an expression of his holy character, to blaspheme it is akin to a personal assault. Further, disobedience to God's commandments may equate to an irreverent disregard for his name, for the law of God is an expression of the character of God: *"If thou wilt not observe to do all the words of this law that are written in this book, that thou mayest fear this glorious and fearful name, THE LORD THY GOD; then the LORD* [Jehovah] *will make thy plagues wonderful..."* (Deut. 28:58-59a).

Jehovah[3], as we will note in the following pages, was the proper name (sometimes called the *nomen ineffabile*, or the "ineffable name") for the God of Israel. During the Hellenistic period, the *tetragrammaton* was deemed so sacred that, in verbal conversation as well as prayer, the Jews substituted the title *Adonai* in its place, and the scribes washed their pens before writing it. But where does such thinking stop? Currently, "Adonai itself has come to be too holy to say for Orthodox Jews, leading to its replacement by HaShem ("The Name")."[4] Again, we might ask, "At what level will efforts to protect the third commandment from potential blasphemy be enough?"

Of course, God never required such prohibitions against the use of his name, or commanded such strict precautions. These kinds of special measures added to the third commandment are typical of the extra layers of protection the Pharisees[5] added to God's law as extra "fences" to avoid violating his commandments (cf. Mt. 15:3-9; 23:16-22). But the Lord revealed

---

[3] יְהֹוָה derives from the formula in Exodus 3:14 ("I am that I am") and is often called the *tetragrammaton* because of the four Hebrew consonants corresponding to the formula—e. g. JHVH or YHWH.

[4] https://en.wikipedia.org/wiki/Names_of_God_in_Judaism

[5] *Halakha* and *Chumra* involved the placement of secondary rules around the Torah (or law of God) to make potential breaches less likely.

this personal, covenant name to them as an expression of his covenant relationship, not as a relic to be protected in a museum behind bullet-proof glass. The way to reverence the Lord's reverend name, in other words, is to take him and his word seriously, not to refuse to use it in verbal conversation. We regard his name as holy when we maintain a spirit of reverential awe before the Lord, exalting him in our thoughts, affections, deeds and words above all that is common, mundane and profane.

Perhaps an illustration will help us to grasp the point. Some years ago, Xerox Corporation bought a full-page ad in the *Wall Street Journal* protesting the popular trend to use the company name as a synonym for all photocopiers. They were tired of people claiming that a document was "xeroxed" when it had been, in fact, reproduced on a Canon, IBM or other brand of photocopier. The ad aimed at distinguishing the Xerox brand as the original, pioneer, trend-setting leader of the market. "We are unique—better than lesser competitors—and no longer want our name used in purely generic terms." That was the message they intended to convey by the ad campaign. Likewise, God is dedicated to the sanctifying of his own name, and we should be too.

Does Pronunciation Matter?

So, though the practice of avoiding the use of his name sounds reverent and pious on the surface, the Pharisees likely went overboard by this self-imposed prohibition not to verbalize the name *Jehovah*. God never commanded them to avoid its use. Likewise, contemporary debate over the correct spelling and pronunciation of the *tetragrammaton*, as well as the even more bizarre emphases of the "sacred name movement,"[6] is similarly

---

[6] The *Yaohushua Organization*, based in Jerusalem, claims to be the only group that knows the true identity of the Creator. They are led by a man identified simply as Cohanul who claims that God gave him a dream/vision in which he revealed that the true name of the Messiah was not "Jesus" but "Yaohushua." The group's website includes numerous statements

unnecessary and distracting. Whether someone spells God's most personal name JHVH or YHWH, and pronounces it *Jehovah* or *Yahweh* is immaterial.

Our current study on the meaning of the three basic Hebrew names for God, together with the various compound names associated with *El* and *Jehovah* (the two most predominant names revealed in the pages of the Old Testament) focuses on the meaning of the Hebrew names, not their respective spellings or pronunciations. That is the more important issue. Allow me to explain.

It has become popular among scholastics over the past few decades to say that the name *Yahweh* is to be preferred to the more traditional name *Jehovah* because, as we are told, the letters "j" and "v" did not exist until circa 1500 A.D., and were not in common use until much later. Now, the question of spelling/pronunciation really doesn't make a big difference one way or the other, but because of the undue emphasis academic types have placed on the issue, I need to say something in defense of my use of the more traditional name *Jehovah* in these pages.

In my opinion, the argument over the pronunciation of God's name is spurious for this reason. Just because a consonant did not exist does not mean the sound represented by the letter was also nonexistent. Even a casual look at an authentic 1611 King James Bible will reveal that certain letters were used to represent numerous sounds. For example, the letter "I" was employed to represent the sounds for *i*, *y*, and *j*, not only in English, but also in

---

indicating that eternal salvation is contingent on the proper use, pronunciation, and response to "the sacred name." This group, like most non-Christian religions (or cults) rejects Biblical inspiration and inerrancy, rejects the perpetuity of the Church, and promotes various ideas (such as, communication with the spirit world, the possibility of demon possession if a person mispronounces "the sacred name," and the ongoing need of performing exorcisms) that mirror the mystery religions. Similar "sacred name" groups, such as the *House of Yahweh,* and *Yahweh's Assembly in Messiah* are also products of the Hebrew Roots Movement.

Hebrew, Greek and Latin. The introduction to the general epistle of James in the 1611 King James Bible, consequently, appeared as follows:

> 1 Iames a seruant of God, and of the Lord Iesus Christ, to the twelue tribes which are scattered abroad, greeting.

> 2 My brethren, count it all ioy when ye fall into diuers temptations.

Are we incorrect then to pronounce the words "Iames," "Iesus," and "ioy" with a *j* sound, and "seruant," "twelue," and "diuers" with a *v* sound? If so, how, pray tell, could preachers possibly communicate with a congregation of worshippers? There is no substitute for common sense when reading the Bible. We must not allow ourselves to be intimidated by self-proclaimed scholars whose primary motive in exposing how Christians have historically gotten it wrong seems to be the undermining of the idea that the Bible is the divinely preserved word of God.

What these supposed linguistic experts fail to tell us is that the letter *y* also did not exist in Biblical Hebrew; consequently, by their own logic, God's name should be *Iahweh*, not *Yahweh*. The bottom line is that the dust storm stirred up by this debate over the correct pronunciation of the "sacred name" leads to chaos and confusion, with no two "experts" arriving at consensus on any one spelling or phonetic articulation.

I suspect that the entire debate is fueled by a failure to distinguish between Biblical Hebrew and Modern Hebrew (or Yiddish), as well as the difference between translating a word and transliterating a word. When the King James translators encountered these names, in other words, they did not actually translate them; instead, they transliterated them, i.e. they represented the letters in the form of the corresponding characters of a different alphabet. Hence, they brought the *tetragrammaton*

יְהֹוָה into the English with the same phonetic sounds and pronunciation of the original language. Whether those letters are JHVH with the implied vowel sounds of *e, o* and *a*, as the ancient Hebrew indicates, or YHWH with the implied vowel sounds of *a* and *e*, as modern Yiddish would suggest, is (again) immaterial, for the pronunciation does not change the meaning of the name. And it's a good thing that it doesn't matter, for no two linguists can seem to arrive at consensus on this issue.[7]

Here is the bottom line: It is always best to trust God's promise to preserve his inspired word. I trust that promise more than fickle, contradictory human scholarship. Just know that it is neither a matter of ignorance nor irreverence to speak of our Lord the way the King James translators have taught us, as *Jehovah* and *Jesus*. I know these precious names, but *Yahweh* and *Yaohushua* are unfamiliar and foreign to my ears.

Why So Many Names?

One further technical issue, by way of introducing this study, is necessary. It is the question "Why does God have so many names in the Old Testament?"

This question is important because various liberal schools of religion[8] have employed this issue in an attempt to undermine the integrity of the Old Testament. Higher criticism argues that the multiple names of God revealed in the Pentateuch (*Genesis, Exodus, Leviticus, Numbers, & Deuteronomy*) prove that it was a human composition, compiled as a sort of anthology from the works of four anonymous authors using various source material. These anonymous "authors" are simply referred to as *J, E, D & P*, for the particular name of God favored by that author. So,

---

[7] As a pastor/teacher, my goal is to communicate God's word as accurately, yet as simply and coherently, as possible; consequently, I see no reason to abandon the old, familiar pronunciation of *Jehovah* for the more modern *Yahweh*.

[8] This school of critical thought goes by different names, such as "Form Criticism," the "Documentary Hypothesis," and the "Wellhausen Theory," popularized by the 19th century German rationalist Julius Wellhausen.

portions of the first five books of the Bible featuring the name *Elohim* were composed, they say, by *E* ("the Elohist"). The passages in which *Jehovah* is the dominant name used were written, according to them, by *J* ("the Jehovist"); *D* stands for the writer of the book of Deuteronomy, according to this school of high criticism, and *P* for the human author of the "priestly" portions of the Pentateuch.

What is the real motive behind this attempt to redefine the Mosaic authorship of the first five books of the Bible? Well, we cannot be certain about personal motives, but there does seem to be an implication that each individual "author," by virtue of specializing on one name more than the other, had a different understanding of who God was, much like a pagan might attribute different attributes to the various gods and goddesses in the pantheon.

"Comparative religion" is the secularist's method of explaining religious history. It suggests that all religion began with *animism*—the belief that a vague spirit resides in trees, rocks and rivers—then evolved into *pantheism, polytheism* and finally *monotheism,* a belief in one God. According to this secular frame of reference, the multiple names of God reflect this evolutionary progress in human history.

How should we respond to these explanations? We reply by remembering four basic facts. First, the Lord Jesus Christ himself affirmed the Mosaic authorship of the Pentateuch (Mt. 19:8; Mr. 1:44; Mr. 12:26; Lk. 24:27; Jno. 5:46); therefore, to cast a shadow of doubt on the actual source of the first five books of the Bible impugns the credibility of the Lord Jesus himself. How can we believe anything Jesus said if he was wrong on this point?

Secondly, Scripture attests to its own divine origin. The Bible is not a mere human production. Though God employed men in the writing of it, he so superintended the process that the words they spoke and wrote are the very words he would have them to speak and write. Theologians call this the doctrine of *verbal* (meaning, the very words), *plenary* (meaning, every word) *inspiration* (cf. 2 Tim. 3:15-16; 2 Pet. 1:20-21). This truth concerning the supernatural origin of Scripture is complemented by multiple promises concerning the supernatural protection of Scripture. The God, in other words, who inspired the Bible has pledged himself to providentially preserve it (cf. Ps. 12:6-7; Ps. 119:89; Mt. 24:35; Jno. 10:35b).

The Bible, in a word, is God's own self-revelation, not a collection of human opinions about God. Even a cursory consideration of various evidences for its supernatural origin—such as the many fulfilled prophecies it contains, its historical accuracy (validated by archaeology, science and history over and again), its pervasive influence on human rights, jurisprudence, economics, medical science, education and every other area of civilization, and its longevity in spite of relentless criticism and attempts to destroy it—should give one pause before adopting the view that it is just another volume in the library of mankind.

Arguments from these liberal scholastics, in other words, or from the professors of Comparative religion, approach the Bible from this anti-supernatural bias. Under the guise of intellectualism, these folk presume to critique God's word, redefining it in purely secular, or naturalistic, terms. They assume that miracles do not exist in order to prove that they cannot occur. But whether they call themselves "scholar," "expert," "professor," or "intellectual," they are nothing more than skeptics and unbelievers. Do not be intimidated by them.

Thirdly, we respond to this explanation concerning the varied names of God by stating that if, indeed, the Bible is God's own self-testimony and revelation, then it follows that the names revealed in its pages are intentional. Each name possesses its own special significance. Just as David may be known as a shepherd, a warrior, a poet, a musician, a king and a prophet, so God is revealed in the Old Testament by these various names, each of which adds another dimension to the unfolding portrait of his glorious Being. We will talk more about this principle, called "progressive revelation," in the next chapter. Suffice it to say now that the Bible writers did not employ these names arbitrarily but with purpose, according to the context. Each new name disclosed a further feature of the character of God.

Finally, we answer this criticism by an important correction. Contrary to the secular paradigm, religious history did not evolve from animism to ancestor worship to nature worship and finally to monotheism. In fact, the story of the Bible is the very opposite of that. Scripture teaches that human history began with monotheism, the worship of the one true and living God, then devolved and degenerated into idolatry via man's sinful mind (cf. Rom. 1:18-32).

What is God's name? Is it *Elohim*? Yes. *Jehovah*? Yes again. *Adonai*? Indeed, it is. Are these multiple gods? Not at all. There is only one true and living God who created all things, who is sovereign over all, who has been pleased to enter into relationship with men, and who makes exclusive claims upon our hearts and lives.

Who is he, then, you ask? Well, stick around, if you will. The final answer may surprise you. And even if it doesn't surprise, it is sure to delight the hearts of all who believe.

1
The Names of God:
Profiles of His Character

"O LORD our Lord, how excellent is thy name in all the earth!" (Psalm 8:1a)

A mong the many reasons I admire and trust the integrity of the *Authorized Version,* or *King James Translation,* of the Bible, is the effort the translators made to distinguish the various Hebrew names of God from one another. To what, you may wonder, do I refer? I am talking about the unique way the KJV translators identified the several names of God in the Old Testament via the use of capitalization.

Have you ever noticed that sometimes the names *Lord* and *God,* in your King James Bible, are printed in all capitals, e. g. *LORD*; *GOD,* while at other times only the first letter is capitalized, e. g. *Lord; God*? Consider Psalm 8:1, the text that heads this chapter. The first mention of the title "Lord" is written in all caps, e. g. LORD, but the second reference to the title in the text is spelled with a capital "L," then a lower-case "o," "r," and "d."

If you are like me, you may have read the Bible for many years before even noticing this unique feature of the KJV. Why does the KJV vary in its use of capital letters when the name of God is written? Is the practice of diverse capitalization simply a matter of random, personal preference? Is there rhyme or reason for the variation? Perhaps, someone conjectures, the discontinuity in capitalization is simply representative of the challenge to achieve consistency in formatting by the publishing company's editor and/or printer. Obviously, one might think, a person cannot expect a volume of substantial size, like the Bible, to be completely free of printing inconsistencies like these.

It may surprise you to learn, however, that the varied use of capitalization of the names "Lord" and "God" in the KJV is intentional. Difference in the use of capital letters is the translators' clue that they have translated one of the three basic Hebrew names for God—*Elohim, Jehovah,* and *Adonai.* For instance, the name *God,* written with a capital "G" and a lower-case "o" and "d," is the Hebrew name *Elohim.* The names *LORD* and *GOD,* written in all capital letters, signal that the translator has rendered the Hebrew name *Jehovah.* And the title *Lord,* printed with a capital "L" and a lower-case "o," "r," and "d," cues the reader to the Hebrew name *Adonai.* The purposeful variation in the use of capitalization is really an ingenious (and honest) way to indicate that the translator has been true to the original text. Again, it is one of the most unique features of the *Authorized Version.*

Appearance in A.V.	**Hebrew Equivalent**
God	*Elohim*
LORD	*Jehovah*
GOD	*Jehovah*
Lord	*Adonai*

What difference does it make, someone wonders? Well, I am so glad you asked. Much would be lost if the translators had failed to be so careful in their treatment of the Biblical text. There is a veritable gold-mine of theological richness in each of these various Hebrew names for God. Had they taken the low-road of convenience and decided to streamline their work in the interest of simply capturing the general sentiment of the text[1], the English speaking world may have very well lost the detail of nuance contained in each of these Divine names.

Consider, for instance, one of numerous passages in the Old Testament where a writer employs several names in close proximity to each other. Psalm 91:1-2 is an excellent example of

---

[1] That is to say, had the translators employed the principle of *dynamic,* as opposed to *formal, equivalence*—an approach that seeks to capture the general idea, but not a "word-for-word" translation…

this practice. Here the Psalmist uses four Divine names in two verses:

> He that dwelleth in the secret place of the most High [*El Elyon*] shall abide under the shadow of the Almighty [*El Shaddai*]. I will say of the LORD [*Jehovah*], He is my refuge and my fortress: my God [*Elohim*]; in him will I trust.

The Psalmist David also uses a variety of Divine names in the 68th Psalm. Verse one speaks of *Elohim*: "*Let God* [Elohim] *arise, let his enemies be scattered...*" Verse four uses *Jehovah*: "*...extol him that rideth upon the heavens by his name JAH* [Jehovah], *and rejoice before him.*" Verse 11 employs the name *Adonai*: "*The Lord* [Adonai] *gave the word: great was the company of those that published it.*" And verse fourteen speaks of *El-Shaddai*: "*When the Almighty* [Shaddai] *scattered kings in it, it was white as snow in Salmon.*"

The 77th Psalm is another example of the intriguing affinity for employing a variety of Divine names in a single setting among Hebrew poets. Asaph asks in verse seven, "*Will the Lord* [Adonai] *cast off forever?*" and in verse nine, "*Hath God* [Elohim] *forgotten to be gracious?*" Then he stops himself in the midst of these queries in verse 10 with a kind of stoic acceptance that his best days were behind him, saying, "*And I said, This is my infirmity: but I will remember the years of the right hand of the most High* [El-Elyon]."

For what purpose did the sacred writers mix and mingle these various names? Were they writing randomly or selecting terms arbitrarily? No; there is nothing random in the practice at all. Instead, the variety, with its use of the particular meaning and nuance attached to each of these different Divine names, adds a variegated richness to the text, like a precious diamond refracts distinct colors from a ray of light.

What is in a Name?

So, what's in a name? In popular culture, a name is seldom intended to be anything more than a label for the sake of identification. But in Scripture, a name is frequently a personal profile or revelation of someone's character. Names were not given willy-nilly, or haphazardly, in Biblical times. In fact, Bible characters were given names that had meaning—names that were more than mere labels for the sake of identification. Sometimes these names were prophecies, in hope that the individual would grow up to reflect the meaning of the name. At other times, the name highlighted a particular personal trait (whether physical appearance, temperament, strength or weakness), significant historical event (cf. 1 Sam. 4:21), or circumstance in which the birth occurred (cf. Gen. 35:18; 1 Chr. 4:9).

Adam, for instance, means "red earth," for he was created from the dust of the ground. *Caleb*, who drove the sons of Anak from Hebron when he was eighty-five years old, means "bold." David's name signifies one who is "beloved," and Gideon's, a "great warrior." *Isaac* means "laughter," *Noah* "rest," *Rebekah* "captivating," *Michael* "like God," *Zipporah* "little bird," *John* "God is gracious," and *Barnabas* "son of consolation, or encouragement."

Frequently, when a person undergoes a significant change or dramatic experience in life, God gives that individual a new name. Jacob's face-to-face encounter with the Angel of the Lord is a striking example of this interesting phenomenon. As day began to dawn, Jacob refused to let the Angel go unless the Angel might bless him. *"And he said unto him, What is thy name? And he said, Jacob. And he said, Thy name shall be called no more Jacob, but Israel: for as a prince hast thou power with God and with men, and hast prevailed"* (Gen. 32:24-28). The name *Jacob* means "supplanter, heel-catcher, trickster" and highlights Jacob's natural penchant for deception and scheming to his own benefit. *Israel*, the new name God gave him, means "prince with God" and suggests the kind of regal future God had planned for him and his increasingly large family.

Likewise, *Abram*'s name was changed to *Abraham* (Gen. 17:5), at a strategically important moment when God confirmed the covenant that he would be a father of many nations, while he was as yet childless. If the name *Abram*, which meant "great father," was embarrassing, the new name *Abraham*, meaning "father of a multitude," would have been even more so, for he still had not had any children. But by faith, Abraham, "*against hope believed in hope that he might become the father of many nations...and being not weak in faith, he considered not his own body now dead, when he was about an hundred years old, neither yet the deadness of Sarah's womb: he staggered not at the promise of God through unbelief; but was strong in faith, giving glory to God; and being fully persuaded that, what He had promised, He was able also to perform*" (Rom. 4:18-20).

Even in the New Testament, we have an example of God changing someone's name to mark the change that his sanctifying power may have in personal character development. *Simon*, one of Jesus' original disciples, certainly lived up to his name, for he was "shifting and unsteady, like sand." Any wind could blow him. But Jesus changed his name to *Peter*, meaning "rock": "*Blessed art thou Simon Barjona, for flesh and blood hath not revealed it unto thee, but my Father which is in heaven. And I say also unto thee, That thou art Peter, and upon this rock will I build my church; and the gates of hell shall not prevail against it*" (Mt. 16:17-18).

So, a name is a *revelation*. It stands for the personality. One of the first questions I ask when meeting a person for the first time is, "What is your name?" And the revelation of the name is a sign of submission, or giving up. It indicates a willingness to be known. When the Angel asked Jacob his name, Jacob complied, but when Jacob returned the inquiry, the Angel refused to surrender that information: "*And Jacob asked him, and said, Tell me, I pray thee, thy name. And he said, Wherefore is it that thou dost ask after my name? And he blessed him there*" (Gen. 32:29).

Interestingly, there is another Old Testament narrative in which this same Angel refused to divulge his name. In Judges 13, a woman is greeted by the Angel of the Lord with the announcement of Samson's birth (cf. Jud. 13:3). When she informs Manoah, her husband, of the unsettling encounter, Manoah prays that God might dispatch the angel again for his benefit. When the angel appeared, Manoah attempted to detain his distinguished visitor with a meal, but the angel refused the invitation. Then Manoah asked, *"What is thy name, that when thy sayings come to pass we may do thee honor? And the angel of the LORD said unto him, Why askest thou thus after my name, seeing it is secret?"* (Jud. 13:17-18). And the angel mysteriously vanished in the fire of the sacrifice to heaven.

The Hebrew word translated "secret" in Judges 13:18 is translated "Wonderful" in Isaiah 9:6. Speaking of the coming Messiah, the prophet says, *"And his name shall be called Wonderful, Counselor, the Mighty God, the Everlasting Father, the Prince of Peace"* (Is. 9:6). We may gather from this that certain Old Testament manifestations of this mysterious character called "the Angel of the Lord" may very well be examples of a *christophany*, or pre-incarnate appearance of the second Divine Person of the Godhead.[2]

But we may also gather from the fact that this mysterious figure refused to divulge His name that the complete and final revelation of God's character would not be given until the Messiah himself was sent into the world. Old Testament revelation of God would, in other words, remain veiled and partially obscure, not open, accessible and complete as it would be when God finally "spoke by His Son" (cf. Heb. 1:3). The Old Testament would provide views of God through the lattice, as it

---

[2] "The Angel of Jehovah" also appears in Genesis 16:13-14, 22:11, 24:7,40, 32:24-32, and elsewhere. Genesis 31:11-14 identifies him as the God of Bethel, and Genesis 48:14-16 as the God who "shepherded [Jacob] all [his] life long and redeemed him from all evil," leading many bible students to conclude that this Angel is none other than a manifestation of Jehovah himself.

were, but His full-orbed glory would not be seen until it might be viewed in "the face of Jesus Christ" (cf. 2 Cor. 4:6).

Why did God withhold a complete disclosure of Himself? Was it because of some reluctance to make Himself known? No; the Lord's cumulative disclosure of His character and counsel is intentional. It is an example of what theologians call the principle of *progressive revelation.*

What is progressive revelation? This theological principle states that God reveals Himself in Scripture "*here a little, there a little; line upon line, and precept upon precept*" (Is. 28:10, 13). As progress is made through the word of God, a complete portrait of the Being of God and His eternal plan of the ages cumulatively develops until it finally culminates in the Person and Work of the Lord Jesus Christ. Proverbs 4:18 expresses this principle poetically, "*The path of the just is as the shining light, that shineth more and more unto the perfect day.*" As each new prophetic detail of the Old Testament is added to previous revelations, the light of holy scripture shines with increasing brilliance and greater specificity toward the One who would be the ultimate manifestation and express image of God's Person (cf. Jno. 1:18; Heb. 1:3). That One would be named *Jesus*, meaning "Jehovah is salvation." This Jesus would say, "*He that hath seen me hath seen the Father*" (Jno. 14:9), for He is the full and final revelation of God.

Prior to that ultimate revelation of God's "name" in the One the prophet identified as "Wonderful," however, God would be pleased to reveal facets of His Divine character by means of various Hebrew names, each rich with meaning and significance. Each of these Divine names is a revelation of a further feature of the essence and character of God. Little by little, God discloses Himself, showing His people by means of each new name another aspect of who He is, what He is like, and how He thinks and acts. This study of the various Hebrew names for God, then, is essentially a survey of the attributes of God. Here is an exercise in the discipline of *theology proper* at a basic and fundamental level.

The Priority of Theology, the Study of God

There is no theme more glorious than the attributes of God. And there is no greater need in this anemic age of God-shrinking[3] than to rediscover the soul-humbling, faith-building, life-changing truth concerning who our God really is.

Why is the recovery of a biblical view of God so necessary today? It is crucial because the superficiality of what passes for modern Christian worship is so pervasive in contemporary culture. "Christianity-lite," like so much of pop-culture, is essentially an attempt to dumb-down the faith to the lowest common denominator. In its pursuit of a more relaxed, casual, seeker-sensitive atmosphere, post-modern "believers" have essentially exchanged the *theocentric* (or God-centered) emphasis of historical Christianity for an *anthropocentric* (or man-centered) focus that is more consistent with the prevailing philosophy of "secularism." An unhealthy subjectivity is the hallmark of our times.

It seems that marketing techniques are of paramount importance in contemporary Christian thought. Everything, from the physical worship structure to the number of members to the cleverness of the speaker to the availability of programs to the popularity of the music to the comfort of the worshippers, hinges on the packaging—on appearances. The pulpit has been replaced by a stage; the split chalice of the sanctuary design, by the atmosphere of a theater; the doctrinally substantive and experientially-rich hymns of the faith, with the endless repetition of praise choruses; the exposition of the word, by an

---

3 Contemporary theologian/author J. I. Packer writes, "Often during the past thirty years, I have found myself publicly lamenting the way in which this twentieth century has indulged unwarrantably great thoughts of humanity and scandalously small thoughts of God. Our time will surely go down in history, at least as far as the West is concerned, as the age of the God-shrinkers." *Rediscovering Holiness*, p. 68.

inspirational, conversational, anecdotal talk of how God wants everyone to be psychologically happy, financially wealthy, and sexually fulfilled. It almost seems that "anything goes" in the quest for numerical growth and a weekly offering sufficient to meet an ever-expanding budget.

Do I exaggerate? I don't think I do. Although there are certainly exceptions to this consumer-oriented, big-business, self-perpetuating, popularity-seeking, people-pleasing model of contemporary church-life, yet it seems to be the rule in more and more cases. I suspect that few truly honest, thinking people today would deny that we have witnessed a radical paradigm-shift in terms of defining church-life and function in our generation.

I write to identify these departures from classical Christianity and to urge readers to rediscover a biblical, God-centered focus not as a matter of personal preference but from the motive of biblical conviction. The church exists in the world as a *"habitation of God through the Spirit"* (Eph. 2:22), that is, a place where He feels at home and indwells the assembly. Her goal is to give God glory *"by Christ Jesus throughout all ages, world without end"* (Eph. 3:21), not to cater to the popular palate or to accommodate the spirit of the age. God intends the church to be a counter-cultural institution, "in but not of the world" (cf. Jno. 17:11,14). Christians are called to be "salt and light" (cf. Mt. 5:13-16), modeling the new standards of heaven's kingdom in a culture governed by the political kingdoms of men.

Nothing is more essential to the integrity and influence of the contemporary church, therefore, than a return to the centrality of Scripture's God-centered emphasis. Theology, the study of God, is the first and most basic business of the church.

I can think of few things that will be a greater catalyst to a genuine spirit of worship and recovery of reverence in the church than a fresh view of the majesty, holiness, sovereignty, fidelity, grace, mercy and love of God. Theology is intended to produce doxology, like eating is designed to produce energy. And nothing will be more effective in the growth of strong, stable, joyful, consistent and productive Christians than a solid, regular fare of God-centered preaching. When He is on display in the public assembly of the church; when mortal men experience weekly encounters with Him as He is proclaimed in the word; when pleasing and obeying and knowing and glorifying Him is set forth as the goal of discipleship, believers are equipped to make a real difference for positive good in their respective, daily lives.

Likewise, nothing will breathe a reviving wind into a person's prayer-life like a sense of the grandeur of the name and character of God. Since prayer is essentially an act of worship and devotion to God (not some kind of mechanical repetition of a magical formula of words, nor self-centered opportunity to present a personal "wish list" like a child circling items in a Christmas catalog), informed reflection on who He is and what He has done with a corresponding attitude of self-humbling and genuine expressions of gratitude and praise should characterize every prayer. The more you know God, the more vibrant will be your time of prayer. More important even that that, your prayers will be more powerful and effective.

In an 1855 sermon on "The Immutability of God," twenty-year old English preacher Charles Haddon Spurgeon emphasized the practical benefits of a study of the attributes of God. He began his sermon with these words:

> "The highest science, the loftiest speculation, the mightiest philosophy, which can ever engage the attention of a child of God, is the name, the nature, the person, the work, the doings, and the existence of the great God whom he calls his Father...It is a subject so vast, that all our thoughts are lost in its immensity; so deep, that our pride is drowned in its infinity. Other subjects we can grapple with; in them we feel a kind of self-content, and go our way with the thought, 'Behold I am wise.' But when we come to this master science, finding that our plumbline cannot sound its depth, and that our eagle eye cannot see its height, we turn away with the thought...'I am but of

yesterday, and know nothing.' No subject of contemplation will tend more to humble the mind, than thoughts of God. But while the subject *humbles* the mind, it also expands it...Nothing will so enlarge the intellect, nothing so magnify the whole soul of man, as a devout, earnest, continued investigation of the great subject of the Deity."

Of all the sciences, or disciplines of knowledge, theology is queen. "*I desired mercy and not sacrifice,*" said God through the prophet Hosea, "*and the knowledge of God more than burnt offerings*" (Hos. 6:6). A man may possess a knowledge of algebra, alchemy, anthropology, architecture, astronomy, or any number of the other very legitimate disciplines of study and learning, but the "highest" of the sciences (as Spurgeon termed it) is the study of God.

Solomon makes this very point in Proverbs 9:10: "*The fear of the Lord is the beginning of wisdom and the knowledge of the holy is understanding.*" Scripture defines ultimate "understanding" in terms of knowing God, the holy One. Every other scientific discipline, whether biology, psychology, physiology, chemistry, sociology, philosophy, law, art, literature, or engineering, is a subcategory of the umbrella science of theology, or the study of God, the first great Cause and last great end of all truth and knowledge. This is the "beginning of wisdom" and if a person does not start here—with the knowledge that He is and that all truth derives from Him—he hasn't even started to be wise or to understand. Theology is the magnetic north of every legitimate scientific investigation and inquiry.

Knowing God's Name

The quest to know God at ever-increasing depths of familiarity, therefore, is the chief end of man and the purpose of his existence. When the Lord Jesus defines "eternal life" in terms of an intimate, relational knowledge of God—"*This is life eternal, that they may know thee, the only true God, and Jesus Christ, whom thou hast sent"* (Jno. 17:3)—he means that the very essence of God's gift of grace to men produces a specific quality of life, the principal feature of which is a rich and fulfilling relationship with the Father and the Son. For those who have been saved, such a pursuit of God is the chief joy and satisfaction of life in this world, and such will be the greatest glory of the next world when we *"know even as also [we] are known"* (1 Cor. 13:12).

The words of Jeremiah 9:23-24, likewise, prioritize the knowledge of God as the overarching goal and purpose of life: *"Let not the wise man glory in his wisdom, neither let the mighty man glory in his might, let not the rich man glory in his riches: but let him that glorieth glory in this, that he understandeth and knoweth me, that I am the LORD which exercise lovingkindness, judgment, and righteousness, in the earth: for in these things I delight, saith the LORD."* Though a person lives his life in relative quietness, obscurity and privation, yet if he knows the Lord, at ever-increasing levels of objective understanding and existential reality, his life is worthwhile, regardless of what judgment others might make of it. There is no higher ambition than to grow in grace and in the knowledge of Jesus Christ the Lord (cf. 2 Pet. 3:18). There is no happier soul than the individual who has God as his portion. There is no greater wisdom than an understanding of His word and conscious awareness of His reality.

The psalmist wrote, *"I have more understanding than all my teachers: for thy testimonies are my meditation. I understand more than the ancients, because I keep thy precepts"* (Ps. 119:99-100). A biblical view of life and the world is true wisdom. No knowledge is more important than a knowledge of the word of God and the God of the word. The individual who possesses such knowledge has greater insight into ultimate truth and reality than the unbeliever, who may in fact be his superior in I.Q. and /or academic achievement.

What are the benefits of knowing the name of the Lord? Psalm 9:10 affirms that such familiarity is the impetus for the act of placing a person's faith in God: *"And they that know thy name will put their trust in thee: for thou, LORD, hast not forsaken them that seek thee."* Daniel 11:32b teaches that the knowledge of God will foster strength and courage in God's people: *"The people that do know their God shall be strong, and do exploits."* Job 22:21 indicates that inward peace results from an experiential knowledge of the character of God: *"Acquaint now thyself with him and be at peace: thereby good shall come unto thee."* And Proverbs 18:10 teaches that an understanding of the name of the Lord is a refuge to the believer in a time of crisis: *"The name of the LORD is a strong tower: the righteous runneth into it, and is safe."*

As we proceed to study the many Hebrew names of God progressively revealed in the Old Testament, perhaps you, too, will discover a quiet haven, safe asylum and boon to your faith in the face of the many trials and challenges of daily life. I know of no exercise more faith-building than reflection on the being and attributes of God. When we see Him high and lifted up, everything else that seemed so monumental and important has a way of assuming its proper shape and size. May the following pages prove to be such a catalyst to your own recalibration of perspective as you read and study.

PART 1

THE PRIMARY NAMES

2
Elohim: The Faithful Creator
אֱלֹהִים

"In the beginning, Elohim created the heaven and the earth." Genesis 1:1

In the beginning, God... There are no more important words anywhere in sacred or secular literature. Every following truth claim, life observation, historical detail and editorial explanation in the Bible depends upon the validity of these four words. If these words are true, they establish a benchmark for measuring truth, reality and ethics—a veritable, philosophical "ground zero," if you please—and set the context in which the entire universe may be explained. If they are false, then the remainder of the Bible is false and religion is the greatest hoax ever perpetrated on mankind. Everything that ultimately matters stands or falls on the integrity of these four words.

Why are these words so important? They are critical to the question of whether or not life is ultimately significant—whether you are just a random assembly of maverick molecules that derived from insignificance and are headed to insignificance, in which case we must all become nihilists and stop caring about anything and everything. After all, if there is no God, then nothing matters...but, then again, it doesn't, does it?...not even the idea of it.

If true, however, these words put us in touch with the one, vital, ultimate reality—the first great Cause of all existence. They define Being. And they do so in terms of One who is the source and origin of everything else.

You see, something must be eternal. By logical necessity, a single, ultimate, eternal Reality must exist prior to and beyond everything else that exists, else the very idea of existence is suspect, and of course, no thinking person (an activity in which both the one who reads this page and the one who now writes it are presently engaged) can deny his own existence.[1] Being must necessarily precede existence.

That fact leaves us with two possibilities. Either matter is eternal—i.e. philosophical materialism—or God is eternal—i.e. biblical theism. Modern science, of course, and its philosophical handmaiden *secularism*, is premised on the idea that matter has eternal being. All that is, the materialist tells us, came to be because two giant meteors hurtling through the space/time continuum collided by chance, the friction of which sparked a simple, biogenetic organism from which everything else evolved over billions and billions of years.

Plausible? Hardly, for the explanation raises more questions than it resolves. Where did the second rock come from? Did the rocks predate the space/time continuum in which they were floating, or did it precede the rocks? Can a spark occur without a charge? From whence, then, did the electromagnetic charge derive? Did the magnetism of the electron precede the formation of the meteor, or was it generated at the moment of the hapless collision? And further, where else, in all of history may it be demonstrated that animate, and especially sentient, life may derive from inanimate matter? Is such a theory even consistent with the most basic law of science—the law of biogenesis, i.e. "life begets life"? May the Darwinian and secular model of origins, then, even be termed "scientific"? Isn't it more akin to philosophy or religion than it is the discipline of science? Further, can matter produce mind? Do rocks think?

Well…apparently they try, but not rationally…or critically…or deductively…or honestly enough to squarely face the consequences of their atheistic ideas.

So we return to the four most important words in the universe: *In the beginning, God…* When everything that is began, God was there. He and he alone is eternal, without beginning, without ending, uncreated, self-existent, and the essence of all that is.

---

[1] Consider Rene Descartes' famous phrase *Cogito ergo sum* ("I think, therefore I am.")

Because He is, the cosmos is orderly, human existence has purpose, the world has meaning, and life matters. And that is just the reason this first and most basic name of God revealed in the Bible is so important.

Who is God?

The first Hebrew name of God we encounter in Holy Scripture is *Elohim* (el'-o-heem), translated **God** in the Authorized Version. It is His most basic, or primary name,[2] and is the name the Lord Jesus employed in the fourth of seven sayings on the cross, transliterated by Matthew, *"Eli, Eli, lama sabachthani?"* (Mt. 27:46a), and by Mark, *"Eloi, Eloi, lama sabachthani? which is, being interpreted, My God, my God, why hast thou forsaken me?"* (Mr. 15:34).

Elohim appears some 2,250 times in the Old Testament, and is the exclusive name used for God in Genesis 1, appearing some thirty-two times. The suffix "im" indicates plurality,[3] meaning "the mighty Ones," and is consequently an early indication in Scripture of the concept that a plurality of Persons exists within the unity of the one God, a doctrine Christianity would later codify in terms of the Trinitarian nature of God.[4]

'El, the root of the name *Elohim*, was originally a common noun employed to speak of the generic concept of supremacy. It suggests an abstract thought, such as someone might refer to a "supreme Being" in modern vernacular. *'El* conveys no concept of personality or relational intimacy or familiarity,[5] expressing

---

[2] The widespread use of the root *'el*, e. g. Beth-el ("house of God"), Isra-el ("prince with God"), Dani-el ("like God"), Samu-el ("asked of God"), etc., shows the predominance of this name in Hebrew culture.

[3] Just as *cherubim* is the plural of the singular *cherub*, and *seraphim* is the plural of the singular *seraph*.

[4] Consider Genesis 1:26: *"Let us* [plural] *make man in our* [plural] *own image, after our* [plural] *likeness."*

[5] *'El "distinguishes him only in his fullness of power without reference to his personality or moral qualities—to any special relation in which he stands to men..."* (Josh McDowell, *Evidence that Demands a Verdict – Vol. II*, p. 122).

only the general idea of transcendence and superiority. The root is even employed to refer to angels in Psalm 29:1 (translated by the word "mighty") and heathen deities (translated by the word "gods" in Exodus 15:11 and 18:11). So, this first name for God with which we meet in the Bible is restricted to revealing simply the most basic and general ideas of His character, i.e. His *"eternal power and Godhead,"* (Rom. 1:20), if you will.

Elohim and the Doctrine of General Revelation

It is generally understood by Bible students that the doctrine of revelation is two-fold. First, God has revealed Himself in nature and creation. We call this "general revelation."[6] Secondly, God has revealed Himself in Scripture. We call this "special revelation." Psalm 19 contains both ideas:

> The heavens declare the glory of God; and the firmament showeth his handiwork. Day unto day uttereth speech, and night unto night showeth knowledge. There is no speech nor language, where their voice is not heard. (Psalm 19:1-3)

Here is the doctrine of *general revelation*.

> The law of the LORD is perfect, converting the soul: the testimony of the LORD is sure, making wise the simple. The statutes of the LORD are right, rejoicing the heart: the commandment of the LORD is pure, enlightening the eyes. (Psalm 19:7-8).

Here is the doctrine of *special revelation*.

---

[6] It is "general" both in terms of its audience and its content. Its target audience is everyone, everywhere ("...there is no speech nor language where their voice is not heard" – Ps. 19:3), and its content is restricted to the general truths that God exists and is powerful. General revelation is partial; it discloses nothing about God's grace in Christ or the covenant of redemption.

Notice that when speaking of the concept of *general revelation*, the first citation—Psalm 19:1-3—exclusively employs the name *Elohim*, signaled by the translators by *God*, with a capital "G" and a lower-case "o" and "d." When addressing the idea of special revelation, however, the Holy Spirit employs the name *Jehovah*, a fact highlighted by the translators by writing the word *LORD* in all caps.

What is the significance of this distinction? I highlight it to say that all men, by virtue of the fact that they are created in the image of God, have some concept of *Elohim*, the most rudimentary revelation of God. General revelation, in other words, is universally accessible, whatever geographic barriers or linguistic differences may exist between one person and another. There is no language where the voice of nature is not heard; the message infiltrates the entire earth, from one end of heaven to the other (cf. Ps. 19:1-6). Even more, everyone gets the message.

Everyone gets the message? Really? Yes…really! In fact, I propose that the universal awareness of *Elohim*'s existence and power is the only legitimate answer to the anthropologist's (and the sociologist's, for that matter) quest to explain the pervasive presence of religion in every ancient and modern people group. Why is every native tribe in undeveloped countries together with the most scientifically-aware and technologically-advanced communities in civilized society intrinsically and categorically religious? Romans 1:18ff provides the answer.

Romans 1 describes the doctrine of natural theology (or general revelation) in precise terms. It answers the question of mankind's religious psyche by saying that, firstly, man has an internal or innate knowledge of God: *"Because that which may be known of God is manifest in them; for God hath showed it unto them"* (Rom. 1:19). Notice the prepositional phrase "in them." Ingrained in the very fabric of man's being as a creature made in God's image is a consciousness that God exists and an inescapable sense that He is there. In other words, a moral law exists within human beings that distinguishes them from all other creatures. He knows, and he cannot escape from that innate knowledge. This is what it means to be human—to be created in God's image.

Notice the phrase "that *which may be known* of God." The knowledge communicated naturally to man is necessarily limited. It is not exhaustive. To be clear, man by nature has no internal or instinctive awareness of specific theological doctrines, such as God's Trinitarian nature, or the virgin birth of Christ, or the principle of substitutionary atonement. These are truths only revealed by special revelation in Scripture.

But he can—and he does—know something about God by nature. He knows that God exists and that this God holds man accountable to a moral standard. By nature, human beings have an internal sense of right and wrong, for they have been created moral beings in God's image. Unlike animals, every human being has a conscience—even those that have so silenced and offended it that they commit "unconscionable" crimes.

Secondly, Romans 1 teaches that God has given such conclusive *external evidence* for His existence in the world that He made so that the individual who does not acknowledge Him is "without excuse": *"For the invisible things of Him from the creation of the world are clearly seen, being understood by the things that are made, even His eternal power and Godhead, so that they are without excuse"* (Rom. 1:20). Note the words "clearly seen." Paul affirms that God may be seen in a very evident way in nature, and understood not only to exist, but also to be extremely powerful and eternal. Paul states in unequivocal terms that creation witnesses so clearly to the existence of God that everybody gets the message! This is common and universal knowledge.

If the concept of general, or natural, revelation is legitimate, then, you may wonder why some people profess atheism. If everyone already knows that God exists, how would Paul explain the existence of atheists? He would answer by saying that man's problem is not an intellectual, but a moral problem. It is not a lack of knowledge but a refusal to acknowledge that which he knows to be true. Paul asserts that people reject God not because they are informationally deprived, but because they have heart trouble. Their depraved hearts are hostile toward God (cf. Rom. 8:7). Even the thought of Him evokes an insidious internal animus. *"The fool hath said in his heart"*—not his head—*"there is no God"* (Ps. 14:1).

The knowledge of God's reality and greatness as it is revealed in nature does, in fact, get through, but fallen man with this insane moral antagonism toward his Creator suppresses it. He *"holds*—the word means "to suppress; to hold back; to hold down"—*the truth in unrighteousness"* (Rom. 1:18b). He so resents God and the fact that he is accountable to Him that rebels against the light of nature: *"Because that, when they knew God, they glorified him not as God, neither were thankful; but became vain in their imaginations, and their foolish heart was darkened"* (Rom. 1:21).

Such is the tragic view of man in sin described in Romans 1. Such a spirit of willful ignorance against even the light of nature shows just how hopeless is the case of mankind apart from the grace of God. If man by nature is so averse to even the most rudimentary facts of God as revealed in creation, then he would never receive or embrace the more comprehensive revelation of God in the gospel. Unless God the Holy Spirit creates within that man a new heart, he will continue to resist and rebel against the very thought of God.

Jehovah: The True *Elohim*

Elohim, then, is the general, or rudimentary, name for God. Every culture has evidence of His existence, greatness and authority, though because of sin men have rebelled against that clear truth and substituted in its place themselves, some bird, four-footed beast or creeping thing as their god (Rom. 1:21-23). Humanity, consequently, is naturally idolatrous, twisting the truth it knows into grotesque forms of paganism and self-worship.

Fallen man refuses to give the true and living God the glory that belongs to Him by acknowledging and worshiping Him.

The Scriptures, however, reveal that the gods of men are really no God at all; instead, *Jehovah* is the true *Elohim*:

- "Among the gods [*'el*] there is none like unto thee, O LORD [*Jehovah*]…" (Ps. 86:8)
- "Now for a long season Israel hath been without the true God [*Elohim*], and without a teaching priest, and without law. But when they in their trouble did turn unto the LORD God [*Jehovah-Elohim*] of Israel, and sought him, he was found of them." (2 Chr. 15:3-4)
- "Thus saith the LORD [*Jehovah*] the King of Israel…I am the first, and I am the last; and beside me there is no God [*Elohim*]." (Is. 44:6)
- "I am the LORD [*Jehovah*], and there is none else, there is no God [*Elohim*] beside me…" (Is. 45:5)

The legendary contest between Elijah and the priests/prophets of Ba-al[7] on Mount Carmel was essentially a showdown concerning the true Elohim. "*If the LORD [Jehovah] be God [Elohim], follow him: but if Baal, then follow him*" (1 Kings 18:21b). How did the competition end? It ended with Baal's silence and a mighty display of Jehovah's glory. The people worshiped saying "*Jehovah is the Elohim; Jehovah is the Elohim*" ("*The LORD, he is the God; the LORD, he is the God*" – 1 Kings 18:39).

Even Cyrus, the heathen emancipator of the Jews from Babylonian captivity, understood that idol gods are really no God at all. He issued this edict for the rebuilding of the Temple in Jerusalem: "*Who is there among you of all his people? his God [Elohim] be with him, and let him go up to Jerusalem, which is in Judah, and build the house of the LORD God [Jehovah-Elohim]*

---

[7] Note the *'el* or *'al* root in the name.

of Israel, (he is the God [*Elohim*],) *which is in Jerusalem*" (Ezra 1:3).

The New Testament church was established in a similar pagan environment to that encountered by the Israelites in Canaan and the greater Mediterranean world. Idolatry was rampant. But Christians, who had received God's special revelation through Christ and the apostles, knew that only one God was the true God. First Corinthians 8:4-7a is the New Testament counterpart to this Old Testament quest to identify the true *Elohim*:

> ...We know that an idol is nothing in the world, and that there is none other God but one. For though there be that are called gods, whether in heaven or in earth, (as there be gods many, and lords many,) but to us there is but one God, the Father, of whom are all things, and we in him; and one Lord Jesus Christ, by whom are all things, and we by him. Howbeit there is not in every man that knowledge...

Though the Jews came to identify the true *Elohim* in personal terms as "Jehovah," and Christians as "God the Father" and "the Lord Jesus Christ," this most basic and fundamental name for God simply expresses the general idea that a supreme Being exists. In a word, the idea of an *Elohim* is more philosophical than personal, more abstract than concrete, more general than specific. As each further name is revealed in the subsequent pages of Holy Scripture, we will discover His specific personality and special relation to man. But Divine revelation starts here, with the simple affirmation that God is and that He is the ultimate Absolute.

Elohim: The Creator of All Things

In more particular terms, what may we learn about God from this most rudimentary name revealed in the Bible? First, we learn that *Elohim* is the Creator God. As previously noted, God is referred to as *Elohim* a total of thirty-four times in the creation narrative of Genesis 1:1 through 2:3. Further, in Solomon's homily to the youth of his day, the Preacher counsels them to *"Remember now thy Creator* [lit. *Elohim] in the days of thy youth, while the evil days come not, nor the years draw nigh, when thou shalt say, I have no pleasure in them"* (Ecc. 12:1). And in Elihu's indictment of people for failing to turn to God in times of calamity, he identifies *Elohim* as man's "Maker": *"But none saith, Where is God [Elohim] my maker, who giveth songs in the night?"* (Job 35:10).

Over and again, this name is connected to the act of special creation:

- "But Jeshurun waxed fat and kicked...then he forsook God [*Elohim*] which made him, and lightly esteemed the Rock of his salvation" (Deut. 32:15).
- "Thus saith God the LORD [*Elohim-Jehovah*], he that created the heavens, and stretched them out; he that spread forth the earth, and that which cometh out of it; he that giveth breath unto the people upon it, and spirit to them that walk therein..." (Is. 42:5)
- "For thus saith the LORD [*Jehovah*] that created the heavens; God [*Elohim*] himself that formed the earth and made it; he hath established it, he created it not in vain, he formed it to be inhabited: I am the LORD [*Jehovah*]; and there is none else." (Is. 45:18)

Further, *Elohim* depicts Him as a *faithful* Creator—a covenant God: *"Know therefore that the LORD [Jehovah] thy God [Elohim], he is God [Elohim], the faithful God [Elohim], which keepeth covenant and mercy with them that love him and keep his commandments to a thousand generations"* (Deut. 7:9).

The etymology of the name *'El* is similar to the Hebrew word *'alah*, [8] which means "to swear." This allusion to the act of

---

[8] Here is the etymological basis of the name *Al-lah* in Islam; hence, we may understand why there is no room in Muslim theology for any idea of a

swearing a covenant oath, or "keeping covenant," emphasizes that the God who created all things is also committed to upholding and preserving His creation. Notice this emphasis on the "faithful Creator" in the following verses:

- "God [*Elohim*] is not a man, that he should lie; neither the son of man, that he should repent: hath he said, and shall he not do it? or hath he spoken, and shall he not make it good?" (Num. 23:19)
- "And he said, LORD God [*Jehovah-Elohim*] of Israel, there is no God [*Elohim*] like thee, in heaven above, or on earth beneath, who keepest covenant and mercy with thy servants that walk before thee with all their heart..." (1 Kings 8:23)
- "For by him were all things created, that are in heaven, and that are in earth, visible and invisible...all things were created by him, and for him: and he is before all things, and by him all things consist" (Col. 1:16-17)
- "...by whom also he made the worlds; who being the brightness of his glory, and the express image of his person, and upholding all things by the word of his power..." (Heb. 1:2b-3a)
- "Wherefore let them that suffer according to the will of God commit the keeping of their souls to him in well doing, as unto a faithful Creator" (1 Pet. 4:19).

The God who made the world, in other words, sustains and maintains the world by the same power with which He created it. He is faithful to the works of His own hands. God is neither remote nor disconnected from the universe that He made, but is personally invested to "uphold" every system on a macro-, and every molecule on a micro-scale. Were *Elohim* to withdraw His

---

relationship between God and man. Consistent with this *'el* root, the sole theological emphasis in Islam is the transcendence and greatness, not the immanence and grace, of God.

sustaining providence from creation for a split second, *"all flesh would perish together"* (Job 34:15).

So, Elohim speaks of God as the God of history. He is the Governor of the world and of all mankind: *"Behold, I am the LORD [Jehovah], the God [Elohim] of all flesh: is there any thing too hard for me?"* (Jer. 32:27). He is great and powerful, the *"Elohim* of heaven" (Dan. 2:44), "the mighty *Elohim"* (Is. 9:6), superior to all, ultimately transcendent over all, yet ruling His world with actual hands-on management. It is no wonder, therefore, that Asaph celebrated this incomparable Creator God, saying, *"Who is so great a God [Elohim] as our God [Elohim]?"* (Ps. 77:13b).

Elohim: The Ultimate "Absolute"

What, then, is the significance of this most basic of the Bible's "big ideas"? I previously noted that the name *Elohim* is a plural noun, meaning "the Mighty Ones." Interestingly, it is always coupled with a singular verb: *"In the beginning, Elohim [plural] created [singular] the heaven and the earth"* (Gen. 1:1). I stated that this blending of plurality and singularity—i.e. of diversity within unity—is an early evidence of the doctrine of the Trinity. The fact that the one true and living God is tripersonal is a truth made conspicuous in the clear light of New Testament revelation.

But there is another lesson we might deduce from this intriguing combination of a plural noun and a singular verb. *Elohim* is what theologians call a "plural of intensity." The plural form of the name suggests the thought that within the fullness of the one God, there is a vastness and infinity that requires comprehensive terms to express it. In a word, *Elohim* depicts the Creator God as the ultimate "Absolute." All the varied dimensions of reality find coherence in the fact of His existence. In *Elohim*, the entire universe is intelligible, life has meaning and purpose, and unity emerges from diversity.

Now I admit that we are presently treading in some deep, philosophical water. But it cannot be helped. The name *Elohim* is essentially philosophical by definition. It answers the basic, philosophical question, "How do all things, as God made them, fit together? Is coherence, order, and a sense of purpose, meaning and significance possible in this wide, wide world? Does a first great Cause exist? Is there such a thing as 'absolute truth'?

This is such a fundamental issue to human existence. It has profound, far-reaching implications. I am confident that the failure to grasp this concept of God as the ultimate "Absolute" is the primary reason people in the modern world feel to be so "lost," and to live such empty, aimless and meaningless lives. As society has become increasingly enamored with modern science (or what Paul calls "science falsely so called" – 1 Tim. 6:20), Darwinists have relentlessly ridiculed the Genesis narrative of special creation (Gen. 1) as ignorant and unscientific, replacing it with the theory of macro-evolution. Secular humanists, sitting at the controls of public education, have successfully expunged every hint of a biblical worldview from school curricula, and implemented programs aimed at deconstructing history of the last vestiges of Christian influence. The result of this radical shift in paradigms—from God's word to human speculation—is that the concept of absolute truth has been replaced by philosophical/moral relativism.[9] "You decide your truth and I'll decide mine" is the mantra of our secular society.

The result is that modern man approaches daily life like a practical atheist. He believes that he came from insignificance and is headed for insignificance. Nothing in the meantime, therefore, ultimately matters. Life has no ultimate meaning. The only thing that matters is the present moment and whatever value the individual chooses to assign to it. To the relativist, there is no ultimate purpose, only purposes. There is no absolute truth, only truths. There is no ultimate beauty, only beautiful things. If there is no God, everything is permissible but nothing really matters.

---

[9] Relativism is the idea that knowledge, truth and morality exist only in relation to current trends in culture or the context of history, and are not absolute.

Is it any wonder that there is such an epidemic of psychological problems in our world? The book of Ecclesiastes defines such a relativistic approach to life in terms of living "under the sun," that is, without any consideration of the God who is above and beyond the sun. And when people live their lives without factoring God into the equation, it produces nothing but "vanity and vexation of spirit." Such a life is an empty sham.

It is worth noting that the phrase "vexation of spirit" means, literally, "chasing the wind." Can you catch the wind? If you could, in fact, track it down, would you be able to seize it? Is it possible to grasp the wind? What a vivid picture of life without God, the ultimate "Absolute"! How many people are pursuing such a fool's errand?

It is to such people that the experienced Preacher tells his young auditors, *"Let us hear the conclusion of the whole matter: Fear God [Elohim], and keep his commandments, for this is the whole duty of man...Remember now thy Creator [Elohim] in the days of thy youth..."* (Ecc. 12:13; 12:1). Only a life lived in the light of *Elohim*'s reality has meaning, purpose, and significance.

Consider an example concerning this point of God's existence as the ultimate reality. Post-secondary education generally takes place in an institution called a "university." A university is a place in which a person may study all the major disciplines in the diverse field of academia, whether biology, chemistry, anatomy, physiology, psychology, sociology, anthropology, mathematics, history, literature, the arts, astronomy, pharmacology, etc.

But have you ever really looked at that word "university." It is a compound word, deriving from the Latin *uni* meaning "one" and *veritas* meaning "truth." Originally, a university was a place where someone might go to learn "one truth."

What was that "one truth"? It was *theology*, the study of God. Theology was once considered "the queen of the sciences." Indeed, the university offered diversity in its academic curriculum, but every specific discipline—again, whether biology, cosmology, paleontology, psychology, economics, law or medicine—was integrated in terms of the ultimate reality, the being and existence of God. Theology was the umbrella discipline beneath which the others were interpreted, the unifying science that made sense of all the rest. Every subcategory of academic study was intended to lead the student back to God the Creator in praise, honor, dependence, and gratitude. It was in the light of God, the ultimate and absolute truth, that unity emerged from diversity and the parts fit together to make the whole.

I think it is safe to say that, as a rule, modern Universities no longer function according to that original paradigm. Perhaps it would be more accurate today to call them "multi-versities" instead, for they have long since abandoned the idea of absolute truth. Now, biology is studied as an end in itself, not as a discipline that derives from *Elohim*, the Source of all life, and returns to Him in adoration and praise. In fact, as Darwin's theory of macro-evolution assumed a posture of predominance among University Professors, biology became the vehicle by which theology and the existence of God was challenged and replaced. The same could be said for the other disciplines. Psychology and economics and history and the arts were redefined in man-centered terms, with self-actualization and self-fulfillment—not the glory of God—the ultimate goal of each.

Relativism produces as many "truths" as there are people to espouse them. Every man is now a self-proclaimed "master of his own fate and captain of his own soul." He worships at the altar of nothing while imagining himself to be something. But he is chasing a mirage and attempting to possess a breeze. It is not surprising that he thinks suicide is the ultimate answer to such a pointless life.

Pop-culture is in a moral free-fall precisely because it has abandoned belief in the Creator God in favor of epistemological and ethical relativism. Without the absolute constructs of truth and error, right and wrong, and good and evil, the chaos of cultural anarchy prevails. Who can witness the public debates over homosexual and lesbian "marriage" and gender-identity, the aggressive push for transgendered restroom facilities in public, the glorification of deviancy and perversion, and every other expression of moral insanity in the civilized world today without seeing that this is what happens when mankind jettisons belief in *Elohim*, the first great Cause and last great End of human existence? It is no wonder that Fyodor Dostoyevsky wrote in *The Brothers Karamazov*, "If God does not exist, then all things are permissible. If there is no God, then there are no rules to live by, no moral law we must follow; we can do whatever we want." Indeed, without this ultimate Absolute—i.e. the being and existence of *Elohim*—all is relative, existential and meaningless. Such a God-less approach to life explains why our world is in the tragic, self-destructive, and chaotic condition it is today.

On the other hand, those of us who approach life acknowledging *Elohim*'s reality and existence as the eternal Absolute find significance and meaning from such sound theology. We know that in this God that created all things for His pleasure and according to His own sovereign will, we "*live, and move, and have our being*" (Acts 17:24-28). His existence is the one, eternal Constant in a world of variables. His absolute reality confers meaning on life and the world, bestows significance and value on the individual, and frames the purpose of life in concrete terms.

Elohim: The Foundation of Reason

This Divine name is further significant in the sense that it explains the reason we live in an orderly, rational universe. *Elohim,* the Creator God, is the basis of reason and logic. Nowhere may we find a better illustration of this than *John* chapter one.

The prologue to John's Gospel (Jno. 1:1-18) is a Christological masterpiece. In what is arguably the most compelling philosophical argument in religious literature, John builds a sequential, indubitable case for the deity of Jesus. By the time he completes the prologue, John has identified the Creator of the universe by the name *Jesus Christ, the only begotten Son, which is in the bosom of the Father* (v. 18).

Why is it significant that he identifies the Creator as a Person? It is significant because John begins the prologue with a description of the Creator in abstract, philosophical terms. He calls Him "the Word" or *Logos*: *"In the beginning was the Word, and the Word was with God, and the Word was God. The same was in the beginning with God. All things were made by him; and without him was not any thing made that was made"* (vs. 1-3).

We derive the idea of "logic" from the Greek *logos*. By calling the Creator *Logos*, John captures the minds of both his Jewish and his Greek readers at the outset of his Gospel. Both would have agreed, at least at an abstract, philosophical level, that there existed a principle of "logic" or rationality in the universe. The Jewish reader would have recalled Psalm 33:6 (*"By the word of the Lord were the heavens made and all the host of them by the breath of his mouth"*) and Proverbs 8 (where the abstract concept of "wisdom" is credited with the act of creation) when he read the word *logos*. The Gentile (or Greek) reader would have instantly thought of the principle of wisdom, reason, logic and order that permeates the created world when he read the word *logos*, for all the great philosophers—Plato, Socrates, Aristotle and the rest—taught that a great Mind of Reason stood in back of the universe and that the structure and order observable in the world testified to that fact.[10]

In my previous title on the *Gospel of John*, I attempted to show how John built a case that the "Word" that created all things is, in fact, Jesus Christ:

"By beginning his gospel with the abstract principle of the *Logos*, John engaged the ear of both his Jewish and his Greek readers. When he says, then, *"In the beginning was the Word, and the Word was with God, and the Word was God"* (1:1), both

---

[10] The Greeks viewed the physical disciplines of mathematics and science as expressions of the metaphysical reality of the *Logos*.

his Jewish and his Gentile auditors would have responded, "Amen." They would also agree with the abstract premise that this Word was the Creator (1:3) and the source of knowledge and enlightenment (1:4 – theologians refer to this as "natural revelation" or "the moral law"—see Ps. 19:1ff).

Verses six through eight (1:6-8), however, mark a dramatic turning point in the case that John is building. In these verses, he moves from the theoretical to the historical – from the abstract to the concrete: *"There was a man sent from God, whose name was John."*

Again, both Jewish and Gentile readers would affirm John's historical point of reference. "Yes," the Greeks would say, for they could not dispute the historical existence of this man named John the Baptist. The Jews also would agree, for they took John to be a true prophet of God.

Verses nine through thirteen (1:9-13) take the argument even a step further as John develops the thought that John the Baptist testified of and pointed to "the true Light." By verse fourteen (1:14), the apostle has set up his readers for an inescapable conclusion. The Word is a Person!

"The Word was made flesh and dwelt among us..." In this verse, John personalizes this abstract concept and states that this "flesh and blood human being" is at one and the same time "the only begotten" Son of God: *"...and we beheld his glory, the glory as of the only begotten of the Father, full of grace and truth."*

Twice in the passage (vs. 14 & 18), John refers to Him as "the only begotten." This combination of adjectives speaks of Him as "the unique One, the one and only, the one of a kind." In contrast to those who are "sons of God" by the new birth (1:13) and those who manifest their sonship by believing (1:12), Jesus is the unique Son of God. He is not God's Son by natural birth, new birth, or special creation, but by virtue of His essential oneness with the Father (cf. v. 18 – "in the bosom of the Father").

Then, in verse seventeen (1:17), John identifies this Incarnate Word who is God's unique Son, and to whom John the Baptist pointed, by the name "Jesus Christ." Verse fifteen (1:15) teaches that the Son (though existing before, yet) came after John the Baptist. Verse sixteen (1:16) identifies the Son as the source of all blessings. Verse seventeen (1:17) names Him "Jesus Christ." Verse eighteen (1:18) identifies Him as co-equal, co-essential, and co-eternal with the Father...

By identifying the Son of God as "Jesus Christ," John implies that everything he has been saying about "the Word" (i.e. the Word is eternal God, the Creator and source of all knowledge) is true about Jesus, and everything he has said about the Son (i.e. the Son is the Word incarnate, the One and only of the Father, the Source of all blessings and the Revealer of the Father) is also true about Jesus.[11]

Elohim, the first and most basic name revealed in the Bible, and *Logos*, John's abstract or philosophical reference to the principle of eternal Reason, are theological synonyms. Both express an identical thought, namely, that the created order is in fact orderly and organized, and this fact points to the fact that it has an Organizer. The intricate design, both at a macro- and a micro-level, presupposes an intelligent Designer. Holy Scripture refers to this Supreme, Rational, Covenant-keeping Creator as *Elohim* in its very first verse.

Elohim: Practically Applied

The Bible, then, starts here. So should we. Special revelation begins with the disclosure that the one eternal God is the Creator of all that exists and the faithful Sustainer of all He created. Without this "big picture" understanding of the Creator God, modern man simply cannot make sense of the universe. Outside the ultimate reality of God's existence, nothing makes sense.

---

[11] Michael L. Gowens, *Expository Essays on the Gospel of John*, pp 4-5.

There is no integrity. In fact, everything *dis-integrates*—philosophically, ethically, culturally, domestically, and personally—if there is no Creator God. There is no ultimate purpose or significance to life in this world. Despair is the only option.

I heard a question recently that illustrated the importance of this ultimate truth. A little child asked her parent, "How do we know what is sinful and what is good? What makes one thing wrong and another thing right?" The perplexed parent went to the pastor with the question but he was just as stumped as the parent. The answer, however, is quite simple. We know right from wrong and truth from error because there is a God. The existence of a good, holy and just God as the only eternal Being and the Source of all that exists is the ultimate benchmark by which everything else in the universe is measured. His nature and character alone, as revealed in nature and grace, is the standard by which all must be judged, for He is *Elohim*.

This revelation of God as *Elohim* is the foundation for all that will follow in the pages of Holy Scripture. It is a rudimentary truth—the most basic of all truths—clearly evident in the world that He has made, intuitive to human nature, and grasped by everyone. Granted, sin has so prejudiced the minds of fallen men as to make them revolt against the light of natural revelation, but they know...and whether or not they like to retain God in their knowledge (cf. Rom. 1:28a), every man still benefits from and uses the rational principles and orderly structure of the cosmos in which he exists.

Every human being, for example, uses the orderly motion of planets to measure time, the polar magnetism of planet Earth to chart a course of travel, the laws of physics to design automobiles, airplanes, watercraft, buildings, bridges and other forms of construction, the ocean and wind currents, barometric pressure and other atmospheric phenomena to predict weather conditions, the plant, animal and mineral kingdoms to discover therapies and cures for disease, the regular transition from one season to the next to plant, harvest and store crops, and many other expressions of an orderly, structured, rational world to navigate his way through life.

With such manifold benefits and expressions of God's goodness (cf. Ps. 145:18) available to mankind in the created order, one may easily understand why the moral rebellion of fallen sinners against this Creator God is so scandalous. The better response to such a good and kind Creator would be to bow before Him in humble adoration and worship. So, *"come, let us worship and bow down: let us kneel before Jehovah our maker. For he is our Elohim..."* (Ps. 95:6-7a).

3
Jehovah: I Am that I Am
יְהֹוָה

"I am the LORD: and I appeared unto Abraham, unto Isaac, and unto Jacob, by the name of God Almighty, but by my name JEHOVAH was I not known unto them."
Exodus 6:2b-3

That the God who created the universe, as recorded in Genesis 1, is the same God that entered into covenant relationship with the Israelites—the predominant theme of the Old Testament—is evident by the appearance of a new name for God in Genesis 2:4: *"These are the generations of the heavens and of the earth when they were created, in the day that the LORD God [Jehovah Elohim] made the earth and the heavens..."* By introducing the name *Jehovah* in Genesis 2, Moses—the sacred penman of Genesis—sets the stage for the story of God's special relationship with the Jewish people that will begin in Genesis 12 and continue throughout the remainder of the Bible.

The revelation of this most personal of Divine names, in other words, was exclusive to the nation of Israel. Though God did not reveal it, as the text heading this chapter indicates, until the time of Moses, yet Moses connects it to *Elohim*, the Creator God, beginning in Genesis 2 to emphasize the fact that he is not describing a multiplicity of separate gods, but one God who is both the Creator of all things in general terms and the Redeemer of the Hebrews in special and particular terms. In other words, the use of *Jehovah* as early as Genesis 2 is an expression of the Holy Spirit's intent to identify the Creator God of the universe—the primary motif of Genesis 1-11—and the Covenant God of the nation of Israel—the Biblical theme beginning with Genesis 12 and following—as one and the same God.

The Origin of the Name

The name *Jehovah,* presented in all capital letters as *LORD* and/or *GOD* by the King James translators, is the most prolific of the Divine names revealed in the Bible. It appears some 6,823 times in the Old Testament and is variously termed God's proper, sacred, and ineffable name. *Jehovah* is the personal and relational name of God. As *Elohim* speaks of God's transcendence (or distance from his creatures), *Jehovah* suggests the thought of his immanence (or nearness) to the people he has claimed as his own. The name is revealed exclusively to the nation of Israel, God's covenant people, and is neither known nor used outside the covenant community.

The name *Jehovah* derives from Moses' experience at the Burning Bush (cf. Ex. 3). Moses, reluctant to assume the role as leader of the exodus, objected that the nation would reject his authority to lead: "And *Moses said unto God, Behold, when I come unto the children of Israel, and shall say unto them, The God* [Elohim] *of your fathers hath sent me unto you; and they shall say to me, What is his name? what shall I say unto them?"* (Ex. 3:13). God replied by revealing this special name: *"And God said unto Moses, I AM THAT I AM: and he said, Thus shalt thou say unto the children of Israel, I AM hath sent me unto you. And God said moreover unto Moses, Thus shalt thou say unto the children of Israel, The LORD God* [Jehovah Elohim] *of your fathers, the God* [Elohim] *of Abraham, the God* [Elohim] *of Isaac, and the God* [Elohim] *of Jacob, hath sent me unto you: this is my name for ever, and this is my memorial unto all generations"* (Ex. 3:14-15).

I AM THAT I AM, then, is God's permanent, personal and proper name. From this intriguing expression, frequently termed the *tetragrammaton,*[1] linguists transliterate the theonym *Jehovah* (or popularly *Yahweh*) as follows:

---

[1] A tetragram consists of four letters.

```
┌─────────────────────────────────────────┐
│                                           │
│     J  e  H  o  V  a  H                   │
│     │     │     │     │                   │
│     I   AM that I   AM                    │
│     │     │     │     │                   │
│     Y  a  H  -  W  e  H                    │
│                                           │
└─────────────────────────────────────────┘
```

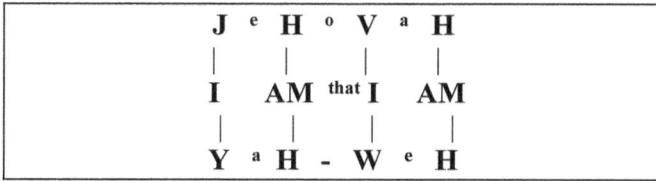

The Definition of the Name

What does the name mean that God gives to himself? *Jehovah* derives from the Hebrew verb *havah* meaning "to be" and speaks of One who has the power of being in himself. The great I AM is the *sovereign, eternally present, redeemer* of his covenant people. Let's explore each of these various nuanced meanings inherent in God's proper name.

First, the name **Jehovah suggests the thought of the sovereignty, or autonomy, of God**. The sovereign God reveals himself as I AM. Faith affirms "He is" (cf. Heb. 11:6) and love exclaims "Thou art!" (cf. Ps. 90:2).

To say that God is sovereign is to say that he has absolute authority. He answers to no one beyond himself, but is his own law, counselor, think-tank, and guide. The prophet Isaiah expresses the thought in terms of a rhetorical question: *"Who hath directed the spirit of Jehovah, or being his counselor hath taught him? With whom took he counsel, and who instructed him, and taught him in the path of judgment, and taught him knowledge, and showed to him the way of understanding?"* (Is. 40:13-14). Obviously, the question is intended to affirm the fact that *Jehovah* is not the beneficiary of education from the school of a superior. He did not derive wisdom or ability or judgment from another, but possesses the power of being within himself as the uncreated essence of all things. He alone possesses plenipotentiary authority.

Paul's classic doxology in Romans 11:33-36 also affirms this thought of essential being, or divine sovereignty: *"O the depth of the riches both of the wisdom and knowledge of God! How*

unsearchable are his judgments, and his ways past finding out!
For who hath known the mind of the Lord? Or who hath been his
counselor? Or who hath first given to him, and it shall be
recompensed unto him again? For of him, and through him, and
to him, are all things: to whom be glory for ever. Amen."

Jehovah, then, is the God that possesses every resource
necessary both for *essence*, i.e. "being," and for *ben essence*, i.e.
"well-being," in himself. Theologians speak of this fact in terms
of the *aseity*, or "self-hood," of God. *Aseity* means that God is
underived, uninfluenced, and unaltered by anything beyond
himself. Nothing external to him has the power to impose or
confer upon him anything that might improve or affect him,
either positively or negatively.

This is the thought intrinsic in Paul's introduction to the
Athenians: *"God that made the world and all things therein,*
seeing that he is Lord of heaven and earth, dwelleth not in
temples made with hands; neither is worshipped with men's
hands, as though he needed any thing, seeing he giveth to all life,
and breath, and all things" (Acts 17:24-25). The God with whom
he is concerned, in other words, is not a beneficiary, but the great
Benefactor of all; not the recipient, but the Source and Origin of
everything else that exists. He "only hath immortality" (cf. 1
Tim. 6:16), being "the King eternal, immortal, invisible, the only
wise God" (1 Tim. 1:17). Everything else has existence from his
Being, not apart from him. He is *havah*, the I AM.

We may further elaborate on this umbrella theme of God's
self-hood, or sovereignty (or aseity, if you please), in terms of
several subcategories. The self-existent *Jehovah* is, by definition,
essentially *self-sustaining, self-determining, self-governing,* and
self-sufficient. Each of these attributes is conveyed by the name I
AM.

The burning bush, out of which God spoke to Moses when
disclosing the *tetragrammaton*, was itself a theophany[2] and an

---

[2] A *theophany* is a visible manifestation of the presence of God, like the pillars
of cloud and fire that guided the Israelites in the wilderness (Num. 9:15-23),

object lesson of the meaning of this name (cf. Ex. 3:1ff). Like the burning bush, *Jehovah* is *self-sustaining*. He expends energy but is not himself expended, consumed or diminished.

Jehovah is also *self-determining* and *self-governing*. When he made the universe, he acted according to his own sovereign pleasure: "*Whatsoever the LORD* [Jehovah] *pleased, that did he in heaven, and in earth, in the seas, and all deep places*" (Ps. 135:6). In fact, every act of the great I AM is a sovereign act: "*But our God is in the heavens: he hath done whatsoever he pleased*" (Ps. 115:3). His decisions are not influenced by external factors: "*But he is in one mind, and who can turn him? And what his soul desireth, even that he doeth*" (Job 23:13). Jehovah is unaccountable to any governing authority beyond himself: "*...that ye may...understand that I am he: before me there was no God* [Elohim] *formed, neither shall there be after me. I, even I, am the LORD* [Jehovah]; *and beside me there is no savior*" (Is. 43:10b-11).

Aseity means also that *Jehovah* is *self-sufficient*. He needs nothing outside himself to complete or fulfill him. Every resource necessary for happiness and satisfaction is contained within himself. Unlike human beings, who need air, water, food and external society, God is self-contained, self-satisfied, and self-fulfilled.

What we are describing here is defined theologically in terms of the immutability of God. The great I AM is not susceptible to change, or mutation. Malachi 3:6 puts it like this: "*I am the LORD* [Jehovah], *I change not; therefore ye sons of Jacob are not consumed.*" Because he is always the I AM, he is necessarily the same in all seasons and circumstances. As the only eternal Being and Source of all that is, *Jehovah* is intrinsically perfect; consequently, he is necessarily immutable. In him, there is "no variableness, neither shadow of turning" (cf. Jas. 1:17).

---

and the burning lamp and smoking flax that passed between the slain animals at the inauguration of the Abrahamic Covenant (Gen. 15:17-21).

Let me explain the significance of this ineffable name in ordinary terms. God's name is not "I was," in the past tense. He is not a "has been." Of course, both this author and many of those who now read these pages are, in a very real sense, "has beens." Someone says, "Back in my day, very few could keep up with me." Or, "You should have seen me in my prime. I could run with the big boys..." or "...I had the features of a top model..." or "...I could work sixteen hours straight without missing a lick..." or "...I could sing like a nightingale...." But ours is a fading glory, isn't it (cf. Is. 40:6-8)? We reach the pinnacle of mental acumen, or athletic prowess, or physical stamina, or personal beauty, but the glory is short-lived. We are unable to sustain the grip on greatness. Our faculties fail us; our focus falters; our talents fade and another takes our place atop the podium. We are left only with a scrapbook of memories and an occasional story, if we can find someone to listen.

But God is the great I AM, in the present tense. He is undiminished, unchanged, unaffected by outside factors. Unlike us, *Jehovah* is never a mere shadow of his former self, but is perpetually and forever the same.

Neither is God's name "I will be," in the future tense. He is not in process of becoming, or improving, or developing. Of course, every young person is an "I will be." A little boy says, "One day, I'm going to play professional baseball or football." A young lady says, "I want to be married one day and have my own family." But now it is not so. There is a process of maturation, growth, and development that must take place prior to the realization of a goal or dream.

Jehovah, on the contrary, is not a work in progress. He is not learning and growing and gaining experience in the matter of Godhood. Instead, he is I AM...already! He has always been I AM and he will always be I AM. That means that whatever an occasion demands, he is up to the challenge; whatever the need may be, he is presently equipped to meet it.

Most grammar teachers would note this statement as an incomplete sentence. The personal pronoun "I" is the subject. The form of be "am" is the verb. But where is the rest of the predicate? I am what? I am hungry? I am smart? I am rich? I am famous? I am what?

But it is not an incomplete sentence so far as God is concerned. Whatever the problem you face, he is the solution. Whatever your need, he can fill it. Whatever your circumstance, he can change it.

In his Gospel, the apostle John records the seven "I am" statements of Jesus. Consider the various predicates the Lord Jesus added to *ego eimi*[3] ("I am..."). Are you walking in the darkness of confusion and ignorance? Jesus says to you, *"I am the Light of the world"* (Jno. 8:12). Are you spiritually hungry? Jesus says, *"I am the Bread of life"* (Jno. 6:35). Are you seeking God and his truth? Jesus says, *"I am the Way, the Truth, and the Life"* (Jno. 14:6). Are you victimized by disease, death and decay? Jesus says, *"I am the Resurrection and the Life"* (Jno. 11:25). Do you feel weak, helpless and vulnerable? Jesus says, *"I am the good Shepherd"* (Jno. 10:11). Do you need help to live productively? Jesus says, *"I am the true Vine"* (Jno. 15:1). Do you seek passage into the safety of the fold? Jesus says, *"I am the Door of the sheep"* (Jno. 10:7). All in all, the addition of direct objects in the New Testament to illustrate what is a complete sentence in the Old Testament, teaches us that the great I AM (and Jesus, who is essentially one with Jehovah, God manifest in the flesh) is capacitated, in and of himself, to meet every need in the lives of his people.

Secondly, the name *Jehovah*, derived from "I AM THAT I AM," **conveys** not only **the idea of God's** sovereignty, but also his **eternal presence**. The account in John 8:51-58 captures this particular nuance.

---

[3] *Ego eimi* ("I am") is the Greek form of the Hebrew *tetragram*.

To the Jews' taunt, *"Art thou greater than our father Abraham, which is dead?"* (Jno. 8:53a), Jesus responded, *"Your father Abraham rejoiced to see my day: and he saw it, and was glad"* (8:56). The Jews retorted, *"Thou art not yet fifty years old, and hast thou seen Abraham?"* (8:57). *"Jesus said unto them, Verily, verily, I say unto you, Before Abraham was, I am"* (8:58). That they understood Jesus' use of *ego eimi* ("I am") as a claim to deity and oneness with *Jehovah* is evident from verse 59: *"Then took they up stones to cast at him..."*

The verb tenses in John 8:58 are insightful: *"Before Abraham was* [past tense], *I am* [present tense]." What is Jesus saying? Someone answers that he was claiming preexistence to Abraham. Well, he was definitely saying that much, but he was doing more than that. Jesus was claiming eternally present preexistence to Abraham. Had he said, "Before Abraham was, I was," he would be claiming preexistence to Abraham. But by saying, "Before Abraham was, I presently am," he indicates that he, as God, is unbound by the limits of time. He presently exists in the past and the future, as well as the present.

Does that trip your mental circuit-breakers? It trips mine as well. Finite brains like ours are incapable of fully comprehending a Being that exists in all times and places simultaneously. By no principle of human logic or familiar benchmark in human experience can we grasp such a concept. It can only apply to the God whose name is the great I AM.

Theologians term this attribute *the omnipresence of God*. At one and the same time, *Jehovah* is everywhere present in all geographical places, time zones, historical and future events. Psalm 139 defines God's omnipresence as follows:

Thou hast beset me behind and before, and laid thine hand upon me...Whither shall I go from thy spirit? Or whither shall I flee from thy presence? If I ascend up into heaven, thou art there: if I make my bed in hell, behold, thou art there. If I take the wings of the morning, and dwell in the uttermost parts of the sea; even there shall thy hand lead me, and thy right hand shall hold me. (Ps. 139:5, 7-10).

No wonder the Psalmist exclaimed, *"Such knowledge is too wonderful for me; it is high, I cannot attain unto it"* (Ps. 139:6)! This name, by which God reveals himself as eternally present, forms a solid bedrock for the integrity of his many promises to be near his people, never leaving nor forsaking them (cf. Jos. 1:9; Is. 41:10; 43:2; Mt. 28:20; Heb. 13:5-6).

Finally, the name *Jehovah* speaks of God as **the Redeemer of his covenant people**. It is a name revealed exclusively to the nation of Israel,[4] not to mankind in general. It teaches that the transcendent Creator, i.e. *Elohim*, is also a God who draws near in relationship to those he loves: *"The LORD* [Jehovah] *hath appeared of old unto me, saying, Yea, I have loved thee with an everlasting love; therefore with lovingkindness have I draw thee"* (Jer. 31:3).

Consider the frequency with which this thought of a covenant relationship appears, especially in Isaiah's prophecy, in connection with the name *Jehovah*.

For I am the LORD thy God [*Jehovah* thy *Elohim*], the Holy One of Israel, thy Saviour…Since thou wast precious in my sight, thou has been honourable, and I have loved thee… (Is. 43:3a, 4a).

Thus saith the LORD [*Jehovah*] the King of Israel, and his redeemer the LORD of hosts [*Jehovah Sabaoth*]; I am the first,

---

[4] In his helpful title *The Names of God*, Andrew Jukes writes: "God had always been 'Jehovah,' but in the character which this name declares, that is, as the God whose love would be in virtue of certain qualities, even His elect, Abraham, Isaac, and Jacob, had not as yet known Him…Not until the redemption out of Egypt, when He gave the law, and said, 'Be ye holy, for I am holy,' was the full import of the name 'Jehovah' revealed to Israel." (pp. 49-50).

and I am the last; and besides me there is no God [*Elohim*] (Is. 44:6).

Surely, shall one say, in the LORD [*Jehovah*] have I righteousness and strength…In the LORD [*Jehovah*] shall all the seed of Israel be justified, and shall glory (Is. 45:24a, 25).

As for our redeemer, the LORD of hosts [*Jehovah Sabaoth*] is his name, the Holy One of Israel (Is. 47:4).

Thus saith the LORD [*Jehovah*], thy redeemer, the Holy One of Israel; I am the LORD thy God [*Jehovah* thy *Elohim*] which teacheth thee to profit, which leadeth thee by the way that thou shouldest go (Is. 48:17).

In a little wrath I hid my face from thee for a moment; but with everlasting kindness will I have mercy on thee, saith the LORD [*Jehovah*] thy redeemer (Is. 54:8).

When the enemy shall come in like a flood, the spirit of the LORD [*Jehovah*] shall lift up a standard against him. And the redeemer shall come to Zion, and unto them that turn from transgression in Jacob, saith the LORD [*Jehovah*]. As for me, this is my covenant with them, saith the LORD [*Jehovah*]… (Is. 59:19b-21a).

This is just a small sampling of the many passages that might be referenced to show the relational nature intrinsic to the name *Jehovah*. It is God's redemptive name, depicting him as the Covenant Keeper (cf. Ps. 136:1; Ex. 33:18-23; 34:5-7). Deuteronomy 4:31 explains Jehovah's covenant commitment to his people succinctly: "(*For Jehovah thy Elohim is a merciful[5] Elohim;) he will not forsake thee, neither destroy thee, nor forget*

---

[5] "Merciful" derives from the Hebrew *chesed*, meaning "covenant loyalty; faithful love, even to the unfaithful."

the covenant of thy fathers which he sware unto them." That, dear friend, is good news.

Summary

Jehovah, then, is the most prolific and personal name of God revealed in the Old Testament. It speaks of him as the sovereign, self-existent, self-sufficient, self-sustaining, self-determining, eternally present, redeemer God who enters into covenant relationship with his people. It derives from the formula revealed to Moses at the burning bush, "I AM THAT I AM," and is his *"name forever, his memorial unto all generations"* (Ex. 3:15b).

It is a name to be reverenced for it is his holy name.[6] It is a name designed to bring comfort, for *Jehovah* has vouchsafed himself in covenant to be our God and to claim us as his people. And it is a name that should evoke songs of praise and fervent worship from our hearts:

> Sing unto God [*Elohim*], sing praises to his name: extol him that rideth upon the heavens by his name JAH[7] [*Jehovah*], and rejoice before him (Ps. 68:4).

Before we consider the third and final of the primary names of God, it may serve to crystallize the relationship between these two predominant names in our minds if we focus a bit more closely on the contrasts between them. This we will do in the next chapter.

---

[6] Consider the duty incumbent upon Moses at the revelation of this name: "Take thy shoes from off thy feet, for the ground whereon thou standest is holy ground."

[7] Notice the frequency with which the "jah" or "iah" root was used in many Hebrew names, e. g. Isa*iah*, Jerem*iah*, Hezek*iah*, Adoni*jah*, Eli*jah*, et al.

4
Comparing the Names

"And of every living thing of all flesh, two of every sort shalt thou bring into the ark, to keep them alive with thee; they shall be male and female... Thus did Noah; according to all that Elohim commanded him, so did he." Genesis 6:19, 22

"Of every clean beast thou shalt take to thee by sevens, the male and his female... And Noah did according unto all that Jehovah commanded him." Genesis 7:2a, 5

It may prove to be very instructive to the bible student when he learns to take special notice of the particular name of God employed at different points in the narrative of Scripture. One fact is certain: Bible writers never use God's name randomly or haphazardly. There is always purpose and significance when they select either the name *Elohim* or the name *Jehovah*.

The historical books of the Old Testament (i.e. *Joshua, Judges, Samuel, Kings*), for example, employ the name of *Jehovah* almost exclusively. The universal books (i.e. *Ecclesiastes, Daniel, Jonah*), on the other hand, predominantly use the name *Elohim*. Furthermore, *Jehovah* dominates Psalms 1-41 and Psalms 85-150, but *Elohim* is paramount in Psalms 42-84. Yet again, as previously noted, *Elohim* takes the principle position in the first eleven chapters of Genesis, but the name *Jehovah* is used almost exclusively beginning in Genesis 12 to the end of the book.

What is the significance of these intriguing facts? In his helpful volume on the *Names of God*, Nathan Stone offers an insightful answer:

"Elohim is the general name of God concerned with the creation and preservation of the world, that is, His works. As Jehovah, He is the God of revelation in the expression of Himself in His essential moral and spiritual attributes. But He is especially, as

Jehovah, the God of revelation to Israel. To Japheth and his descendents, He is the Elohim, the transcendent Deity, but to Shem and his descendents, through Abraham and Isaac, He is Jehovah, the God of revelation."[1]

This distinction between the general and the specific—between the relationship God bears to all men as their Creator and the special relationship he bears to his covenant people as Redeemer—is, without doubt, the motivation behind the particular use of each name in the Old Testament. Even a cursory look at the two passages that head this chapter, i.e. Genesis 6:19, 22 and Genesis 7:2a, 5, will serve to illustrate this point.

The Genesis 6 passage, for example, couples *Elohim* with the command to take two of every living animal—a male and a female—into the ark, for as Creator, God is committed to the preservation and maintenance of the world that he has made. By way of contrast, the Genesis 7 passage employs the name *Jehovah* in connection with the more specific command to take "clean," that is, *kosher* (or sacrificially and dietetically acceptable), animals into the ark by sevens, in male/female pairs. Why is the name *Jehovah* used in connection with the gathering of animals considered to be ceremonially clean? Because the concern now is not merely the preservation of creation but the worship of God.

How do we know that Divine worship is the motive behind the command to take clean beasts in groups of seven, the male and his female? Anyone with a third grade education in mathematics knows the answer, for two is not a factor of seven. Seven animals, consisting of male/female pairs, of each "clean" kind, consists of three male/female pairs, with one animal left over. What is the purpose of the extra animal? Sacrifice.

Genesis 8:20 indicates that after the flood waters receded, *"Noah builded an altar unto Jehovah; and took of every clean*

---

[1] Nathan Stone, *Names of God*, p. 22.

beast, and of every clean fowl, and offered burnt offerings on the altar. And Jehovah *smelled a sweet savour…"* The extra clean animal was intended for the Divine worship, not merely natural preservation; therefore, the command to take clean animals by sevens is attributed to *Jehovah,* for *Jehovah* is the redemptive name of God.

That this explanation is correct may be supported by the argument that in the first seven chapters of Leviticus, the name *Elohim* appears as a stand-alone Divine name only once (Lev. 2:13),[2] though *Jehovah* appears eighty-six times. What is the significance of the overwhelming predominance of the name *Jehovah* and the conspicuous absence of the name *Elohim* in these chapters? The first seven chapters of Leviticus set forth the system of sacrifice and ceremonial offerings prescribed for Divine worship; hence, the covenant, relational name of God appears almost exclusively.

The Structure of *Genesis*

Perhaps the most notable example in which the Holy Spirit transitions from the use of *Elohim* to *Jehovah* in the sacred text is the difference between *Genesis* chapters one through eleven and *Genesis* chapters twelve and following. It is *Elohim* that created all things (Gen. 1), looked upon the earth and saw it was corrupt (Gen. 6:11-13), remembered Noah and every living thing, making a wind to assuage the waters (Gen. 8:1), sent Noah out of the ark after the flood (Gen. 8:16), and established the covenant to never again destroy the earth by water (Gen. 9:8ff).

It is *Jehovah,* however, that called Abram to depart from his homeland (Gen. 12:1), made a covenant with Abraham (Gen. 15:17ff), appeared to him in the plains of Mamre as he sat in the tent door in the heat of the day (Gen. 18:1), revealed to him his intention to destroy Sodom and Gomorrah (Gen. 18:17ff), visited Sarah so that she conceived (Gen. 21:1), prospered Abraham's

---

[2] It also appears in connection with *Jehovah* in Lev. 4:25.

servant as he went to fetch a bride for Isaac (Gen. 24:56), confirmed the covenant to Isaac at Beersheba (Gen. 26:23-25), confirmed the covenant to Jacob at Bethel (Gen. 28:10-15), and sustained Joseph in Egypt (Gen. 39:2, 5, 21-23).

Granted, there are exceptions to this rule in Genesis. The name *Elohim* is not exclusive to Genesis 1-11, nor the name *Jehovah* to Genesis 12-50. That a transition is evident beginning with chapter twelve is significant, however, for it is in Genesis 12 that the Old Testament's "main event" begins, namely God's covenant purpose for Abraham and his seed. In a previous title, I wrote these words:

> The Old Testament, consisting of thirty-nine books, is basically a story within a story—a sub-plot developed within a larger context...redemptive history framed against the backdrop of secular, or world, history. Genesis sets the larger context for the development of the Divine plot in the first eleven chapters. Here we learn that God, as Creator of the universe, exercises sovereign authority in history...It is within this broad context of world history that Genesis 12 begins to sketch the details of redemptive history. Think of Genesis 1-11, then, in terms of a telescope, and Genesis 12 and following in terms of a microscope. Genesis 1-11 offers us the broad-spectrum, wide-angle setting of the Biblical story. Genesis 12, however, narrows the focus and shines the Divine spotlight on the minutia of God's plan for a specific people—the nation of Israel, popularly called the Hebrews or the Jews...The story of the Old Testament, then, is the account of God's special plan for the Jews set within the broader context of His more general plan for the world.[3]

This structure of the book provides rationale for the transition in divine nomenclature. *Elohim* is paramount in Genesis 1-11 because it is the name associated with world history; *Jehovah*

---

[3] *Understanding Your Bible: An Old Testament Survey*, pp. 1-3.

holds the top spot beginning in Genesis 12 and following because it is the name especially associated with the Jewish people and the developing plot of redemptive history.

The Book of *Jonah*

Another portion of Old Testament scripture that reveals purpose and motive in the use of the two primary Divine names is the book of *Jonah*. This book, filed within the section known as "the Minor Prophets," is closer to a personal memoir, or narrative of a particular experience in the prophet's life, than it is a prophecy. It reads like a series of entries in Jonah's personal diary.

It is the story of Jonah's revolt against a Divine assignment that he considered to be totally unreasonable. And before we judge him too harshly for the folly of thinking he could successfully revolt against God, it may be wise to consider that very few people, faced with a similar commission, would not be tempted to respond in the same way.

Does it sound like I believe Jonah was justified to rebel against the call of God? I don't believe that. What he did was wrong...and foolish. But Jonah's commission was not the kind of task to which Jewish prophets were commonly drafted. Let me explain.

Jonah was a Jewish prophet commissioned to prophesy against the Assyrian empire. It was difficult enough to announce God's coming judgment against his own Jewish people, but he was tasked with the unpalatable assignment of denouncing a foreign empire, who neither knew Jonah nor Jonah's God. Of course, it is one thing to accept criticism from one of your own, but an outsider with no vested interest in those he presumes to verbally castigate is seldom tolerated for long. This assignment must have seemed impossible to Jonah.

Secondly, unlike Obadiah and Nahum, the only other prophets called to deliver a message of coming judgment to people outside the covenant people of God,[4] Jonah was tasked with the responsibility to deliver his "in your face" message in person. At least Obadiah and Nahum had the pleasure of denouncing foreign kingdoms in writing. Jonah had to do so—not via snail mail, email, or proxy messenger, but—personally and directly.

Can you imagine the personal danger such an assignment would necessarily involve? It would be comparable to a modern Jewish rabbi traveling alone from Tel Aviv, Israel to Tehran, Iran, and setting out on foot at one end of the city all the way to the other, denouncing the Iranians and their Islamic religion, and threatening them with certain judgment from the God of the Hebrews. Who could possibly undertake such an assignment and expect to keep his head attached to his body?

Jonah, indeed, had ample incentive to dread such an unpleasant assignment. Again, before we judge him too harshly, we likely need to examine whether or not we would not have shrunk from the same task had God given it to us. I cannot think of another Jewish prophet, either previous or subsequent to Jonah, called to such a hard assignment, i.e. to deliver, in person, a Divine malediction to ignorant, hostile foreigners. We can be sure they were none too thrilled to encounter this unsolicited outsider who criticized them so stridently.

Now, the fact that the men of Nineveh worshiped pagan gods raises a very important question: On what basis could the Hebrew prophet Jonah speak authoritatively to a nation that neither knew nor acknowledged Jehovah? Jonah's authority derived from the fact that *Jehovah* is the *Elohim* of all mankind. In fact, he is "the God [*Elohim*] of all nations" (Ps. 22:28).

Although these nations were not privy to the covenant blessing of special revelation like the Jews (cf. Rom. 3:1-2), they were, nonetheless, beneficiaries of God's creation blessings, i.e. natural

---

[4] Obadiah's prophecy was addressed to the Edomites; Nahum's, like Jonah's, was addressed to the Assyrians, approximately a century after Jonah. Isaiah is a third Jewish prophet also given a message for foreign empires (cf. Is. 13-23), albeit as a subplot in his larger prophecy against his own Jewish people.

life, breath, food, water, etc. (cf. Mt. 5:45; Lk. 6:35b; Ps. 145:9, 14-17), as well as the general revelation of God's moral law both in the natural world and in the human conscience (cf. Rom. 1:19; Ecc. 3:11; Pro. 20:27). Interestingly, the book of Jonah carefully delineates between God's general relationship toward all men as Creator and God's special relationship toward Jonah and the Hebrews as Redeemer by deliberately transitioning between the names *Elohim* and *Jehovah* in the inspired narrative.

Consider Jonah chapter one. It was "the word of *Jehovah*" that called Jonah to visit Nineveh (1:1). Further, the narrative reveals that Jonah fled "from the presence of *Jehovah*" (1:3), and *Jehovah*, in turn, that "sent out a great wind into the sea...so that the ship was like to be broken" (1:4). When the shipmaster awoke Jonah, however, he bade him to "arise, call upon thy *Elohim*, if so be that *Elohim* will think upon us that we perish not" (1:6). Upon inquiry of the cause of the storm, Jonah explained to his shipmates, "I am an Hebrew: and I fear *Jehovah*, the *Elohim* of heaven, which hath made the sea and the dry land" (1:9). Once Jonah identifies God by the name *Jehovah*, the sailors prayed unto him for mercy, feared him, and offered sacrifice unto him (1:14-16).

Jonah 1:17 introduces the next chapter by saying, "Now *Jehovah* had prepared a great fish to swallow up Jonah. And Jonah was in the belly of the fish three days and three nights." Throughout Jonah chapter two, then, the name *Jehovah* is used almost exclusively. As Jonah stood on the banks of deliverance, he freely confessed that it was *Jehovah*, not his own effort or ingenuity, that saved him: "Salvation is of *Jehovah*" (2:9).

Chapter three begins with the record of *Jehovah*'s second commission to Jonah: "And the word of *Jehovah* came unto Jonah the second time..." (3:1). This time, Jonah obeyed (3:3). As he entered the city, Jonah announced that judgment would fall in a mere forty days. It is intriguing that the narrative transitions at this point from the use of the name *Jehovah* to *Elohim*: "So the people of Nineveh believed *Elohim*, and proclaimed a fast...And [the king] caused it to be proclaimed and published through Nineveh...Let man and beast be covered with sackcloth, and cry mightily unto *Elohim*...Who can tell if *Elohim* will turn and repent, and turn away from his fierce anger, that we perish not?" (3:5, 7, 8, 9).   Chapter three concludes with this editorial comment: "And *Elohim* saw their works, that they turned from their evil way; and *Elohim* repented of the evil, that he had said that he would do unto them; and he did it not" (3:10).

It is significant that these heathen Assyrians dealt with God not as *Jehovah* but as *Elohim*. And it is further significant that the editorial in 3:10 indicates that it was *Elohim* that responded to the city's repentance. What, someone asks, is the significance of this fact? It suggests that no covenant relationship exists between the people of Nineveh and the Lord. The moral law of God as Creator of all mankind is the sole basis on which he deals with them, and they with him.

This fact, i.e. that the inhabitants of Nineveh had no covenant relation to Jehovah, but rather only a Creator/creature level of accountability, provides the answer to the perennial theological question, "What was the nature of their repentance?" It is not uncommon to hear men claim that Jonah preached to the men of Nineveh and "the whole city repented and got saved." But was this an example of a city-wide revival in which the whole city "got saved"?

I suggest that the specific use of the Divine names in this book prove that this chapter has nothing whatsoever to do with eternal salvation. Though what happens after a person dies and where that individual spends eternity is an issue of ultimate importance, it isn't the only subject addressed in the bible. The message of God's word cannot simply be reduced to a message about where a person will spend eternity. Scripture is not only concerned with the subjects of heaven and hell.

The fact that the name *Elohim* is employed exclusively in the narrative of how the people of Nineveh responded to Jonah's preaching (as noted previously) suggests that this was not a redemptive transaction. The question here is not whether these people were children of God. Instead, Jonah 3 is an episode in which the Creator of all mankind calls his creatures to account for their many abuses of his moral law. Jonah did not preach the gospel—a definitive message concerning the person and work of Jesus Christ (cf. 1 Cor. 1:23a)—for there was no mention of the cross, or justification by an imputed righteousness, or the finished work of redemption. Instead, he preached a message of "judgment to come," much like Paul preached to Felix (cf. Acts 24:25); consequently, the repentance of Nineveh was not evangelical, or gospel, repentance, but a national reformation designed to delay the execution of Divine justice.

Furthermore, the fact that their repentance didn't last—for in a mere thirty years, the Assyrians would invade and conquer Jonah's homeland, the northern kingdom of Israel, and in another seventy, the prophet Nahum would be sent to the same city to telegraph the city's certain destruction as a Divine judgment—is another argument that eternal salvation is not the subject in view, as preachers sometimes suggest, in Jonah 3.

At best, the repentance of Nineveh when Jonah preached to them is comparable to what happened in America in the aftermath of 9/11/2001. The whole nation reacted to the trauma of terror attacks by returning to church and praying. For almost an entire month, church buildings were filled and mention of God was common in the public square. In short order, however, the temporary intensity of religious interest faded and the nation resumed its ordinary secular mood and approach to daily life. Nineveh's repentance was really nothing more than a temporary "stay of execution."

Jonah 3 simply reminds us that God, as Creator, holds nations, cities, families, and churches accountable before his moral law, judging them when they rebel against him. Consider the many examples of temporal judgments, i.e. judgments with present, not eternal, consequence, in Scripture. The Bible teaches that God judges individuals (cf. Rom. 14:12; Col. 3:25), families (cf. Ex.

17:14; 1 Sam. 3:12), local churches (cf. Rev. 2-3), particular cities (cf. Gen. 18; Mt. 11:20-24), nations (cf. Ps. 9:17; 22:28; Pro. 14:34; Jer. 20:7), and culture in general when it rebels against him (cf. Genesis 6-9). Jonah 3 is an example of God's temporal judgment on a city and the nation of which it is the capital. When one compares the dichotomy in this passage between the specific use of *Jehovah* (when the narrative concerns Divine communication to Jonah), and *Elohim* (when God's relation to the Assyrian empire is in view), it is supremely theologically instructive. The chapter teaches that God bears a relation to all mankind as Creator (*Elohim*), holding them accountable before him, but only to his covenant people as Redeemer (*Jehovah*).

Other Examples

Other examples of cases in which the Holy Spirit inspires the Bible writer to predominately use *Elohim* when we might expect him to use God's personal name *Jehovah* are the books of *Ecclesiastes* and *Daniel*. Why do these books prefer the more general over the personal name for God? The answer is likely associated with the intended audience of these books.

Ecclesiastes is classified among Old Testament "wisdom literature." King Solomon, whose political influence spread far beyond the parameters of his own empire, was renowned throughout the Mediterranean world for his wisdom. The case of the Queen of Sheba who traveled a great distance to consult with him was likely not an isolated incident. It is probable that King Solomon was in demand as a counselor on an international level.

It is not surprising, therefore, that Solomon's homily (or sermon)[5] employs the more general name for God for the message of *Ecclesiastes* contains general wisdom for life, not specific revelation for divine worship. The target audience is

---

[5] Ecclesiastes bears all the marks of a formal oration, or homily. Solomon refers to himself as "the Preacher" (1:1), and employs exhortatory language to his auditors throughout.

clearly mankind in general, not the Jewish people in particular. The book addresses the broad-sweeping philosophical question of the meaning and significance of life, a question that is at the very center of what it means to be human.

Solomon's sermon has a text: *"Vanity of vanities, saith the Preacher, vanity of vanities; all is vanity"* (1:2). After announcing this rather depressing theme, he proceeds to develop the text by showing the utter emptiness and meaninglessness of life "under the sun," i.e. without God factored into the equation. Solomon would have agreed with Paul who defined the purpose of man's existence in terms of pursuing the Creator that made him: "...*And* [God] *hath made of one blood all men for to dwell upon all the face of the earth...that they should seek the Lord, if haply they might feel after him, and find him, though he be not far from every one of us"* (Acts 17:26a, 27). Life is intended for God's glory, not for self-indulgence. That's the message of *Ecclesiastes.*

What is the setting for delivering this grim sermon? The repeated references to death and the grave indicate that Solomon wants his hearers to think of him delivering this sermon in a cemetery. He intends to hit them hard with the ultimate reality that death is the great leveler. Over and again he reminds his auditors that "one event happeneth to" both the fool and the wise man—death (2:14-17; cf. 3:19-21; 5:15-16; 9:4-6, 12; 12:3-7). Though the tone is dark and dismal, Solomon is giving his audience a hefty dose of reality.

To whom in particular does he direct his message? Who is his audience? Solomon is addressing young people. Notice the references to youth in the book: *"Rejoice, O young man, in thy youth; and let thy heart cheer thee in the days of thy youth..."* (11:9); *"Remember now thy Creator in the days of thy youth, while the evil days come not, nor the years draw nigh..."* (12:1). The aged Preacher offers to his youthful auditors the benefit of his own experience. If they will listen to him, they will spare themselves much heartache and regret.

So, this is a message for humanity concerning the meaning and purpose of life. It is fitting, therefore, that Solomon exclusively employs the name *Elohim*, "the Creator God," throughout the book. Life without God is futile and empty, he insists. The only life that is worthwhile is a life lived with a view to pleasing and honoring God by obedience to his commandments (cf. Ecc. 12:13). That's the conclusion to the whole matter.

Likewise, the name *Elohim* predominates in the book of *Daniel*. Though Daniel is a Jewish prophet, he is living in Babylon. His book contains both narrative of important events and prophecies of the future. The use of *Elohim*, as opposed to the special and personal name *Jehovah*, is likely due to two important factors: (1) The Jews were captives of the heathen Babylonians, far from Jerusalem, and the true worship of *Jehovah* in Solomon's temple had ceased in 586 B.C.; (2) *Daniel* reveals that God intends to judge Babylon for her sins and to display his sovereign authority over every political kingdom.

The book of *Daniel* teaches that God rules in the kingdoms of men, even over Babylon, and plans to display the superiority of his kingdom in history. It is this kingdom motif (with its contrast between the political kingdoms of men and the historical establishment of the kingdom of God) that makes the use of *Elohim*, the more general and universal name for God, especially significant in this book.

As previously stated, God's covenant name *Jehovah* is prominent beginning with the story of Abraham in Genesis 12, and is the most expressive and personal of God's names. But as a general rule, *Elohim* appears in cases of God's interaction with non-Jewish people, and when the focus is more universal and generic. Understanding this basic dichotomy is a key to insightful study of this intriguing theme.

5
Adonai: Lord and Master
אֲדֹנָי

"In the year that king Uzziah died I saw also Adonai sitting upon a throne, high and lifted up, and his train filled the temple." Isaiah 6:1

A*donai*, the third and final of the most prominent Hebrew names for God is more of a title than a name. It is translated *Lord[1]* some 340 times in the King James Version. Unlike the names *Elohim* and *Jehovah*—names that describe characteristics of God's nature— *Adonai* emphasizes the relationship in which he stands to man.

Interestingly, like *Elohim, Adonai* is a plural proper noun, indicating the Trinitarian nature of God. In cases where it appears in an intra-Trinitarian conversation, however, the singular is employed. Psalm 110:1, for example, reads, *"The LORD said unto my Lord, Sit thou at my right hand, until I make thine enemies thy footstool."* Literally, the verse says, *"Jehovah* said unto my *Adon...,"* in the singular.

The Meaning of *Adonai*

The first occurrence of this name is Genesis 15:2: *"And Abram said, Lord GOD* [Adonai Jehovah], *what wilt thou give me, seeing I go childless, and the steward of my house is this Eliezer of Damascus?"* By employing this compound name, Abraham acknowledges that *Jehovah,* his Redeemer, is also *Adonai,* his Master, and expresses both submission to and reliance upon *Adonai.* Here we learn that *Adonai* is a title of respect and honor. It speaks of God as the sovereign King, the ultimate authority or one in charge.

---

[1] In the King James Bible, *Adonai* is signaled by the use of a capital "L" and lowercase letters "ord."

The name actually carries a dual meaning. It means both "master" (or "lord") and "husband." It pictures two familiar relationships: (1) the relationship of a master to his servant (or slave), and (2) the relationship of a husband to his wife. Intrinsic to this title *Adonai*, then, is the thought of hierarchy with its attending authority/submission dynamic.

Of course, modern man dislikes any structure that places one person into a subordinate position to another; nevertheless, the principle of hierarchy is built into the very fabric of creation. Psalm 8:5-8 describes the order of authority in the world that God made:

> For thou hast made him a little lower than the angels, and hast crowned him with glory and honor. Thou madest him to have dominion over the works of thy hands; thou hast put all things under his feet: all sheep and oxen, yea, and the beasts of the field; the fowl of the air, and the fish of the sea, and whatsoever passeth through the paths of the seas.

Paul further develops this principle of natural hierarchy in 1 Corinthians 11:3:

> But I would have you know, that the head of every man is Christ; and the head of the woman is the man; and the head of Christ is God.

It is clear that this hierarchy in the natural world is not an arrangement based on personal value or importance, but functionality. Without some functional structure, no relationship can survive without degrading into chaos and anarchy. A multiple-headed entity is a monstrosity, and all of nature—from a colony of ants to the food chain—operates on the principle of some structure of authority and submission. An egalitarian world, at least at a structural level, is essentially a self-defeating arrangement.

The New Testament affirms the legitimacy of the principle of hierarchy, both in terms of the master/servant relationship and the husband/wife relationship. In Ephesians 6, Paul writes to Christians who serve under the authority of a master, and who occupy a position of authority over a subordinate, to remind them of what it means to behave Christianly in that relationship:

> Servants, be obedient to them that are your masters according to the flesh, with fear and trembling, in singleness of your heart, as unto Christ; not with eyeservice, as menpleasers; but as the servants of Christ, doing the will of God from the heart; with good will doing service, as to the Lord, and not to men: knowing that whatsoever good thing any man doeth, the same shall he receive of the Lord, whether he be bond or free. And, ye masters, do the same things unto them, forbearing threatening: knowing that your Master also is in heaven; neither is there respect of persons with him. (Eph. 6:5-9).

It is significant that he does not excuse them from mutual responsibility to function within this hierarchy simply because they share a belief in the gospel and love for Christ in common. Instead, he urges each party to fulfill his particular role in the hierarchy as an act of devotion to the Lord Jesus Christ.

In terms of the husband/wife relationship, Peter similarly urges his readers to function within a domestic hierarchy with an eye to the Lordship of Christ:

> For after this manner in the old time the holy women also, who trusted in God, adorned themselves, being in subjection unto their own husbands: even as Sara obeyed Abraham, calling him lord: whose daughters ye are, as long as ye do well, and are not afraid with any amazement. Likewise, ye husands, dwell with them according to knowledge, giving honor unto the wife, as unto the weaker vessel, and as being heirs together of the grace of life; that your prayers be not hindered. (1 Pet. 3:5-7).

Christian liberty, then, is no justification for rejecting these authority/submission roles that are such an indigenous part of the natural world. In fact, the very opposite is true. The believer in Jesus is called to embrace the God-given hierarchy as an act of obedient devotion to Christ as Lord (or *Adonai*).

What are the implications of the name *Adonai* to humanity? What attitudes should the fact that God is Lord, the ultimate Authority, elicit from us? ***First, Adonai speaks of God's possession.*** He has exclusive rights of ownership to every creature; therefore, an attitude of submission to his authority is the only appropriate response.

If God is *Adonai*, he holds claim by right of creation upon every aspect of the lives of his subjects. Their respective hearts, souls, minds, and very beings belong to him and him alone (cf. Mt. 22:37-38). For those also embraced in the everlasting covenant, God exercises ownership not only by the right of creation but also by right of purchase, or redemption: *"What? Know ye not that your body is the temple of the Holy Ghost which is in you, which ye have of God, and ye are not your own? For ye are bought with a price: therefore glorify God in your body, and in your spirit, which are God's"* (1 Cor. 6:19-20). A slave is not his own, but the property of his master. Likewise, because God is *Adonai*, the only acceptable response from mankind is to humbly acknowledge with the Psalmist, *"I am thy servant; give me understanding, that I may know thy testimonies"* (Ps. 119:125).

Secondly, Adonai speaks of God's position. He occupies a position of ultimate authority; therefore, an attitude of reverence before his superiority is always appropriate. If the Psalmist advised inanimate nature to "Tremble, thou earth, at the presence of *Adonai*, at the presence of the *Elohim* of Jacob" (Ps. 114:7), then such a reverent response to the sovereign Lord seems especially appropriate from sentient creatures like man. *"The fear of Adonai,"* that is, the kind of respectful attitude a person might have toward one who is his superior, *"that is wisdom; and to depart from evil is understanding"* (Job 28:28).

Thirdly, Adonai speaks of God's provision. Because of his position as the sovereign, *Adonai* assumes responsibility to care for his subjects; therefore, an attitude of dependence and reliance upon him is the only appropriate response. Popular culture tends to view every master/slave relationship as something negative and oppressive, but that is not the case in the Bible. Scripture depicts the master/slave relationship in positive and personal terms. A master may exercise authority without becoming a despot and a slave may submit without servile fear. The best masters assume responsibility for the protection and provision of their subjects. The best servants respond with an attitude of reverential awe that issues in complete obedience (*vis a vis*, the nature of interaction between Abraham and his servant, Eliezer). As Lord and King over his subjects, God our *Adonai* takes great concern for the welfare of all under his sovereign sway. In a word, far from suggesting some kind of tyranny and cruelty, *Adonai* couples the thought of authority with loving care and concern, like a husband protecting his bride; like a master making provision for his servant (cf. Ps. 123:2).

Adonai in Scripture

What is the significance of this name as it is used in Scripture? One of the most striking discoveries is to note how God's people turned instinctively to this name in trying times. The name *Adonai* assured them of the help they needed to fulfill their appointed service and vocational callings.

In Isaiah 6 for example, the text that heads this chapter, Isaiah is given a vision of the heavenly throne inhabited by *Adonai* at the moment when the throne of Judah had been vacated by the king's demise: *"In the year that king Uzziah died, I saw also the Lord* [Adonai] *sitting upon a throne, high and lifted up, and his train filled the temple"* (v. 1). Nathan Stone comments on this strategically important event:

His earthly lord and master had died, but what does that matter
when the Lord of lords, the Adonai in the heavens, lives and
reigns. This Adonai is seated upon a throne too, but high and
lifted up, above all earthly lords and monarchs...This vision of
God as Adonai started him out on his prophetic career.[2]

Uzziah was one of the godly kings of Judah. He was also one
of the longest reigning kings, having sat on the throne for fifty-
two years. No doubt, to many of the people in his kingdom,
Uzziah was the only king they had ever known. But his godly
focus notwithstanding, Uzziah died under Divine judgment. He
lived the last decade of his life a leper, quarantined from society
in solitary confinement, because he had presumed to usurp the
role of the priests in offering incense before the Lord. His death,
then, struck a tragic note and left the nation perplexed about the
future. "Where do we go from here?" must have been the
question uppermost in the minds of the people as they grappled
with the vacuum left by the king's demise.

But Isaiah saw that even though Uzziah was no longer on his
throne, *Adonai* was still the sovereign ruler of heaven and earth.
The throne of the universe was still occupied; therefore, he and
the nation as a whole had adequate reason to move forward. How
wonderful to know that when earthly leaders fail us, our Lord and
Master yet reigns as King over his kingdom!

Likewise, in the Psalms, King David employs this name in his
own prayers to his greater Lord and King. In Psalm 35:22-23, for
instance, David appeals to *Adonai* for help against his enemies:
"*This thou hast seen, O LORD* [Jehovah]: *keep not silence: O
Lord* [Adonai], *be not far from me. Stir up thyself, and awake to
my judgment, even unto my cause, my God* [Elohim] *and my Lord*
[Adonai]." And in Psalm 38, he acknowledges *Adonai* as his
salvation in trouble: "*Lord* [Adonai], *all my desire is before thee;*

---

[2] Nathan Stone, *Names of God*, pp. 48-49 (Moody Press: Chicago, 1994).

and my groaning is not hid from thee...For in thee, O LORD [Jehovah], *do I hope: thou wilt hear, O Lord* [Adonai] *my God* [Elohim]...*Make haste to help me, O Lord* [Adonai] *my salvation"* (vs. 9, 15, 22). Also, in Psalm 40:17, he finds comfort in the fact that *Adonai* takes knowledge of his case: *"But I am poor and needy; yet the Lord* [Adonai] *thinketh upon me: thou art my help and my deliverer; make no tarrying, O my God* [Elohim]."

The reality of the thrilling title exercises a salutary effect upon the hearts of God's children in this world. He is the sovereign Lord of heaven and earth; consequently, we may depend upon him to protect us, provide our needs, and defend us against those who would harm our souls in this world. *Adonai* is the King by sovereign right. As such he has the right to impose his claims upon our lives and we should learn the privilege of living in subjection to his authority. Further, as Lord and King, he has pledged himself in covenant commitment to provide for and protect his subjects; therefore, we must busy ourselves in the matter of doing his bidding while depending upon him to care for our every need.

The Old Testament *Adonai* and the New Testament *Kurios*

This Old Testament title finds its parallel in the New Testament Greek word *kurios*, translated "Lord." The term is used in Matthew 10:24-25 where Jesus explains the principle of hierarchy: *"The disciple is not above his master, nor the servant above his lord* [kurios]. *It is enough for the disciple that he be as his master, and the servant as his lord* [kurios];" and in John 13:13-14: *"Ye call me Master and Lord* [kurios]: *and ye say well; for so I am. If I then, your Lord* [kurios] *and Master, have washed your feet; ye also ought to wash one another's feet."* Like *Adonai*, the title *Kurios* speaks of a relationship in which both the responsibility of accountability to Christ (cf. Col. 4:1) and the privilege of being protected by him (cf. 2 Tim. 4:18) are involved.

The early Christian confession *Iesous ho Kurios*, i.e. Jesus is Lord (cf. 1 Cor. 12:3; Phi. 2:11), therefore, is not only an acknowledgement of Christ's deity, but an act of willing submission to his authority over one's life. The willingness to bow before him, owning his right to rule one's life is the distinguishing mark between the church and the world. The church is comprised of people who have bowed the knee to the Lordship of Jesus Christ.

In fact, the very term "church" derives from the title *kurios*. Of course, we have Anglicized this English word by using the soft "ch" sound. In Scotland, however, a church is called a "kirk." Do you see the similarity between *ch-ur-ch* and *k-ir-k*? Interestingly, the term "kirk" is an abridgement of the Greek word *kuriake* (from the root *kurios*) which means "belonging to the Lord."

What is a church? It is an assembly of people who belong to the *Kurios*. The popular author Andrew Jukes writes about the fact that the willingness to acknowledge and submit to Christ as Lord (or the sovereign authority) is the point of divide between the church and the world:

> The name Adonai teaches that a relationship answering to that of servants to their lord, and of wives to their husbands, exists between God in heaven and His creature man upon the earth. Not only do the elect, in their approaches to Him, constantly use this name in addressing God, to express their relation to and dependence on Him, as well as their faith in the faithfulness of One, who, because He is their rightful Lord, is bound to sustain, and keep, and help them; but God also no less, when speaking of Himself, continually claims this title, as declaring His relationships of Master and Husband to us – relationships, which, while they set us in the place of honor, for to be even a servant, much more to be the beloved, of the King of kings is great honor, no less involve most solemn responsibilities, if,

called with such a calling, we are unfaithful to it. *In nothing more therefore than in the confession or denial of this name do we see the radical contrast between the church and the world. The church is the church because it acknowledges this relationship: the world is the world because in practice it denies it.* The great mark of the elect is that they 'know the Lord,' while the world yet knows Him not, and acts as far as may be in independence of Him. The world's way is to do as it likes, think as it likes, speak as it likes, without regard to any higher will above it. Its great ones do 'according to their will.' They say 'Our lips are our own: who is lord over us?' They live as if they were their own...The very opposite marks all God's saints. [They ask] 'Lord, what wilt thou have me to do?' ...for they know that not in self-will, but in God's will, and in it alone, is perfect rest.[3] [emphasis mine]

The right response to this exalted name *Adonai*, then, is a willing submission to God as Lord and King over our lives. Though man by nature revolts against the government of God over his life (cf. Ps. 2), the church consists, by definition, of people who have ceased to fight against God and seek their own way, and have come to the point of happy subjection to his claims upon their lives. Their primary concern in every matter is *"Lord, what wilt thou have me to do?"* (Acts 9:6a), for they recognize that they are not their own but belong to the Lord. Their attitude at all times is *"Speak, Lord, for thy servant heareth"* (1 Sam. 3:9). They are people under authority and glad to be counted as such.

Paul regularly referred to himself as a *"bondslave of the Lord Jesus Christ"* (cf. Rom. 1:1; Phi. 1:1; Titus 1:1). In his mind, such a position was the ultimate privilege, affording true freedom and fulfillment. It was "the Lord" that had placed him into the ministry (1 Tim. 1:12; Acts 20:24), and "the Lord" who had

---

[3] Andrew Jukes, *The Names of God*, pp. 113-114 (Kregel Publications, 1984).

sustained him in such (2 Tim. 4:17). It was "the Lord" who opened doors for the success of the gospel (2 Cor. 2:12), and "the Lord" who directed the course of his gospel labors (Acts 16:10).

Jesus Christ is Lord of all. That is a fact. But the question we must ask ourselves is, "Have I acknowledged his lordship over my heart, mind, words, deeds, attitudes, relationships, and every other area of life?" One day, every knee will bow and every tongue confess his lordship to the glory of God the Father (cf. Phi. 2:11). Until then, the church exists in this world as people who belong to this Lord and gladly own him as their King even now. May every heaven-born person join Thomas in his confession of Christ, saying, *"My Lord and my God."*

PART 2

COMPOUNDS OF *ELOHIM*

6
El-Shaddai: **Almighty God**

"And when Abram was ninety years old and nine, Jehovah appeared to Abram, and
said unto him, I am the Almighty God; walk before me and be thou perfect."
Genesis 17:1

It had been almost a quarter of a century since God called
Abram from Ur of the Chaldeans and gave him the promise
that he would have a son. Of course, waiting for twenty-five days
for a desired prospect is not easy to do; and waiting for twenty-
five months is an even greater challenge to faith. But waiting for
twenty-five years to see a promise fulfilled must have felt like an
eternity.

Abram means "great father." I'm sure it was embarrassing
when introducing himself to someone as Abram to have to
answer the question, "How many children do you have?" When
he replied, "I don't have any children," the next question was
sure to be, "Then why is your name 'Abram'?" Now, twenty-five
years after God promised him a son, he must have wondered if he
might have misunderstood the promise. I mean, he wasn't getting
any younger. And Sarai his wife was not only barren but now,
past the age of childbearing.

It was no easy thing, then, when God changed his name from
Abram to Abraham (cf. Gen. 17:5). If Abram, meaning "great
father," was embarrassing, Abraham, meaning "father of a
multitude," was even more so, for as yet he still had no children.
To encourage his faith, however, God also reveals, for the first
time, his own new name: *"I am the Almighty God"* (Gen. 17:1b),
or to transliterate the Hebrew, "I am *El-Shaddai*."

The Divine name *El-Shaddai* appears forty-eight times in the
Old Testament, thirty-one of which are in the book of *Job*.[1] It was

---

[1] This is one of many arguments for dating the life of Job in the time of the
Patriarchs. It is likely that Job was a contemporary of Abraham, explaining the

prominent in the days of the Patriarchs: "*I appeared unto Abraham, unto Isaac, and unto Jacob, by the name of God Almighty* [El-Shaddai], *but by my name JEHOVAH was I not known to them*" (Ex. 6:3). As an example of its patriarchal use, consider Isaac's blessing to Jacob as he sent him away to take a bride: "*And God Almighty* [El-Shaddai] *bless thee, and make thee fruitful, and multiply thee, that thou mayest be a multitude of people...*" (Gen. 28:3).

The Meaning of *El-Shaddai*

The etymology of the Hebrew name *Shaddai* is not definitive, but linguists tend to agree that it likely derives from two possible sources, each of which provides a dramatic picture. The first is a picture of a mountain, possibly derived from the Aramaic word *shadu*, meaning "mountain." Like the visceral sense of intimidation a person experiences when standing at the base of a towering mountain peak, or like the physical power of a volcanic eruption, *El-Shaddai* dwarfs and overpowers everything else.

This image of "the Overpowerer" is certainly consistent with the English translation "Almighty." That *El-Shaddai* is the all-powerful God, or the God who is able to work his will and fulfill his promise is the message God intended to convey to Abraham in the revelation of this name in Genesis 17:1. "Yes, it has been twenty-five years since I promised you a son," God says to Abraham, "but I am able to fulfill my word." Discussing this episode in Romans 4, the apostle Paul puts special emphasis on the power of God to work in a situation that appeared to be impossible:

And being not weak in faith, [Abraham] considered not his own body now dead, when he was about an hundred years old, neither yet the deadness of Sara's womb: he staggered not at the promise of God through unbelief; but was strong in faith, giving glory to

---

prominence of *Shaddai* in *Job*.

God; and being fully persuaded that, what he had promised, he was able also to perform. (Rom. 4:19-21).

The overwhelming power of *El-Shaddai* is also invested in protecting his people, like a towering mountain shelters a traveler in the storm: "*He that dwelleth in the secret place of the most High shall abide under the shadow of the Almighty* [Shaddai]" (Ps. 91:1). Nothing is too hard for our Mighty God.

The second picture is derived from the Hebrew word *shad*, meaning "breast." It is the picture of a nursing mother. It is likely that the English verb "to shed" comes from this Sanskrit root. Like a nursing mother who supplies every need of her hungry, restless child, *El-Shaddai* sheds forth his grace and supplies every needed resource for his children (cf. Is. 66:10-13; Ps. 36:8). *El-Shaddai* is able to quiet the restless and nourish the needy. Like a mother who pours herself out for her little one, so *God Almighty* pours himself out for his people (cf. Ps. 81:10; Jno. 1:16, 18; Acts 2:33).

This rich name, then, not only suggests the thought of Divine power and ability, but also of all-sufficiency. In the Septuagint,[2] the Hebrew name *Shaddai* is frequently translated by the Greek *ikanos*, meaning "all sufficient." *El-Shaddai* is the bountiful God, or the God who is, in and of himself, sufficient for every need in the lives of his children. He possesses an inexhaustible bounty— or, as John Newton put it, a "never failing treasury filled with boundless stores of grace."[3] No need we face is ever beyond his Divine resources. No problem we encounter is ever greater than his Divine power.

Both metaphors intrinsic to this name—the overpowering mountain and the nourishment supplied by a devoted mother— appear together in several places in Scripture. Consider, for

---

[2] The Septuagint, or the LXX, is the Greek translation of the Old Testament.
[3] "How Sweet the Name of Jesus Sounds," John Newton, *Olney Hymns: Book I, No. LVII*

example, Jacob's dying blessing on the patriarch Joseph in
Genesis 49:25-26:

> [Joseph's] hands were made strong by the hands of the mighty
> God [*Elohim*] of Jacob...even by the God [*Elohim*] of thy father,
> who shall help thee; and by the Almighty [*Shaddai*], who shall
> bless thee with the blessings of heaven above, blessings of the
> deep that lieth under, blessings of the breasts, and of the womb:
> the blessings of thy father have prevailed above the blessings of
> my progenitors unto the utmost bound of the everlasting hills:
> they shall be on the head of Joseph, and on the crown of the head
> of him that was separate from his brethren.

Notice how Jacob mixes the "mountain" metaphor with the
"nursing mother" metaphor as he elaborates on the "help" that
will be given to Joseph by *El-Shaddai*. Agrarian people, like the
patriarchs, perceived blessing to come down from the mountains
because it was the mountain streams that fed the rivers which
watered their fields and vineyards. The Psalmist's resolution to
"look unto the hills from whence cometh [his] help" (cf. Ps.
121:1) suggests the same idea. Likewise, Moses' blessing before
his death on the tribe of Joseph employs the identical imagery:

> And of Joseph he said, Blessed of the LORD [*Jehovah*] be his
> land, for the precious things of heaven, for the dew, and for the
> deep that coucheth beneath, and for the precious fruits brought
> forth by the sun, and for the precious things put forth by the
> moon, and for the chief things of the ancient mountains, and for
> the precious things of the lasting hills, and for the precious things
> of the earth and fulness thereof, and for the good will of him that
> dwelt in the bush: let the blessing come upon the head of Joseph,
> and upon the top of the head of him that was separated from his
> brethren (Deut. 33:13-16).

This bountiful God is still "Almighty" today: *"I am Alpha and Omega, the beginning and the ending, saith the Lord, which is, and which was, and which is to come, the Almighty"* (Rev. 1:8). All that is true of *El-Shaddai* as known and trusted by the patriarchs is still true for us.

Application

What practical lessons may we glean from the revelation of this Divine name? What are the implications of the name *El-Shaddai* to us? We might list three specific applications of this sublime name.

First, consider the folly of "taking on" *El-Shaddai*. No one can contend with the Almighty and win. When Naomi returned to Bethlehem-Judah after a ten year detour in the land of the Moabites, now bereft of her husband and both sons, she responded to inquiries about her dramatically aged appearance by saying, *"Call me not Naomi, call me Mara: for the Almighty* [Shaddai] *hath dealt very bitterly with me. I went out full, and the LORD* [Jehovah] *hath brought me home again empty: why then call ye me Naomi, seeing the LORD* [Jehovah] *hath testified against me, and the Almighty* [Shaddai] *hath afflicted me?"* (Ruth 1:20-21).

Likewise, at the conclusion of the first round of God's "whirlwind" reply (cf. Job 38:1 – 39:30) to Job's indiscreet appeal in his own defense, he queried, *"Shall he that contendeth with the Almighty* [Shaddai] *instruct him? He that reproveth God* [Elohim], *let him answer it"* (Job 40:2). Job then confesses he had spoken precipitously: *"I will lay mine hand upon my mouth. Once have I spoken; but I will not answer: yea twice; but I will proceed no further"* (Job 40:4b-5). Then a second wave of cyclonic assault from *El-Shaddai* begins in Job 40:6. This new barrage of rapid-fire, staccato interrogatories lasts until the end of chapter 41, leaving Job completely defeated and humbled (cf. Job 42:1-6).

Secondly, take courage in knowing that nothing is too hard for *El-Shaddai*. As the weeping prophet Jeremiah presided over the sad scene of Jerusalem's fall, the Lord comforted him with a promise of restoration, even though such a prospect seemed impossible at the moment: *"Houses and fields and vineyards shall be possessed again in this land"* (Jer. 32:15b). At this unlikely promise, the prophet responded with this doxology of faith: *"Ah, Lord GOD* [Adonai Jehovah]*! Behold, thou hast made the heaven and the earth by thy great power and stretched out arm, and there is nothing too hard for thee...the Great, the Mighty God* [El-Shaddai], *the LORD of hosts* [Jehovah-sabaoth] *is his name, great in counsel, and mighty* [shad] *in work..."* (Jer. 32:17-19a).

Our Almighty God possesses the necessary resources to accomplish his purposes. There are few exercises more helpful to flagging faith than a fresh look at the many "God is able" verses in Scripture. The next time you find yourself struggling with doubt and fear, take a few moments to seriously reflect on these precious gems—to "ponder anew what the Almighty can do":

- If it be so, *our God whom we serve is able* to deliver us from the burning fiery furnace, and he will deliver us out of thine hand, O king. (Dan. 3:17)

- And the king spake and said to Daniel, O Daniel, servant of the living God, *is thy God, whom thou servest continually, able* to deliver thee from the lions? Then said Daniel unto the king, O king, live for ever. (Dan. 6:20b-21)

- Now unto *him that is able* to do exceeding abundantly above all that we ask or think, according to the power that worketh in us... (Eph. 3:20)

- Who shall change our vile body, that it may be fashioned like unto his glorious body, according to the working whereby *he is able* even to subdue all things unto himself. (Phi. 3:21).

* I know whom I have believed, and am persuaded that *he is able* to keep that which I have committed unto him against that day. (2 Tim. 1:12b).

* Wherefore *he is able* also to save them to the uttermost that come unto God by him, seeing he ever liveth to maketh intercession for them. (Heb. 7:25)

Knowing God as *El-Shaddai* gives every believer reason to exclaim *"Alleluia: for the Lord God omnipotent reigneth"* (Rev. 19:6b). Nothing is impossible with our Almighty God (cf. Lk. 1:36-37).

Finally, find comfort in the truth that *El-Shaddai* is your sufficiency. His powerful resources have been pledged to your preservation, protection and empowerment, until time is no more: *"But my God shall supply all your need according to his riches in glory by Christ Jesus"* (Phi. 4:19). What a thrilling promise!

Of course, before a person finds any solace at all in this truth, he/she must first realize his own utter insufficiency and inadequacy. By nature, man boasts of his self-sufficiency. "I don't need God or anyone else to help me," he proudly affirms. But it doesn't take much real-life experience to teach us that life and the world is too big for us—that we cannot solve every problem on our own, or handle every burden without assistance. The journey of life is too great for us (cf. 1 Kings 19:7). In fact, if we are honest, we must acknowledge that it doesn't take very much pressure or disappointment to knock us off the perch of personal peace and sanity. Most people are much more fragile than they like to admit, or perhaps even realize.

To the individual humbled by life's pressures and responsibilities, however, what great relief is found in abandoning self-sufficiency, confessing personal insufficiency, and exchanging a self-absorbed life for the life of faith—a life that rests in God's "all-sufficiency"! It is a great paradox, but there is no happier day in a person's life than the moment he finally confesses, "I am not adequate for the task at hand," for then, and only then, may that individual find resolution for every necessity of life in the character of God.

El-Shaddai has the sufficient resources to sustain you in the midst of life's trials. His word to Paul, struggling with the thorn in his flesh, is also his word to every burdened soul: "*My grace is sufficient for thee*" (2 Cor. 12:9). Whatever your need may be, it will never be greater than God's available resources to meet that need. He is enough for every one of his children, no matter the test, come what may in their respective life experience.

El-Shaddai is also adequate for those who are called to minister and serve him. He has the needed resources to enable preachers (and every believer, for that matter) to fulfill their respective responsibilities. Paul models the right attitude for every gospel minister, as well as the divine perspective necessary to faithful service: "*Not that we are sufficient of ourselves to think any thing as of ourselves; but our sufficiency is of God*" (2 Cor. 3:5). To every pastor who has ever felt overwhelmed by the weight of pastoral responsibility, God would say, "Remember, I am *El-Shaddai*."

7
El-Roi: The God Who Sees

"And she called the name of the Lord that spake unto her, Thou God seest me: for she said, Have I also here looked after him that seeth me? Wherefore the well was called Beer-la-hai-roi..." Genesis 16:13-14a

Most of the Divine names in Scripture are self-revelations of God, but a few, like *El-Roi*, are names ascribed to God by people.[1] That means, necessarily, that these names do not appear outside the specific narrative in which they originated; nevertheless, each conveys a sublime truth affirmed in the larger testimony of God's word.

El-Roi means "God sees." It was ascribed to God by Sarai's Egyptian handmaid, Hagar. The circumstances in which Hagar attributed this unique name to the Lord are extremely enlightening. The story may be found in Genesis 16.

At Sarai's behest, Abram took Hagar to produce a child on behalf of his barren wife (Gen. 16:1-3). When Hagar discovered that she had conceived, however, the lowly servant-girl adopted an air of superiority toward Sarai, her mistress. Understandably, Sarai reacted harshly to her servant's arrogance, and Hagar ran away into the wilderness, probably intending to return to Egypt (vs. 4-6).

Sarai's severe treatment of her was nothing compared to the perils Hagar would face in the desert. The pregnant woman would be exposed to extreme conditions, both during the scorching heat of daylight and the frigid temperatures each night. Scarcity of food and water meant that her very survival was in jeopardy. Perils of wild animals, human predators, sand storms, and the rough terrain made the prospect that she would reach home very doubtful. But somehow she discovered an oasis in the

---

[1] Other names ascribed to God by people, including *Jehovah-jireh, Jehovah-nissi,* and *Jehovah-shalom,* will be discussed in successive chapters.

desert and sat down to rest beside it. It was there that the angel of the LORD appeared to her (v. 7).

Use your sanctified imagination and ask yourself how she must have felt at that moment. The pain of recent rejection, coupled with the indignity of pregnancy without a husband and not the faintest prospect of future happiness, Hagar must have felt profoundly alone. Is it not reasonable to think that she wondered if even God cared for her plight?

It was to the forlorn exile that the angel of *Jehovah* appeared with two probing questions, *"Whence camest thou? And whither wilt thou go?"* (v. 8). These questions required her to face both the indiscretion and the impracticality of running away from her problems. Then the Lord charged her to return to Sarai with a better attitude (v. 9), and promised to bless her with numerous descendents (v. 10). Finally, he gave her specific instructions about the child she carried: *"Behold, thou art with child, and shalt bear a son, and shalt call his name Ishmael; because the LORD* [Jehovah] *hath heard thy affliction. And he will be a wild man; his hand will be against every man, and every man's hand against him; and he shall dwell in the presence of all his brethren"* (vs. 11-12).

Ishmael, the name the angel gave to the child she carried, means "God hears." God had indeed heard her affliction. He cared for her plight. He was concerned about the hapless slave girl. In a jubilant response of fresh hope, Hagar called the name of *Jehovah* that spoke to her, *El-Roi*, "God sees me."

Notice that God is not only the God who sees; he is the God who sees *me*. *"Thou God seest me,"* said the encouraged woman (v. 13a). And perhaps for the first time in her life, she had also seen him: *"...for she said, Have I also here looked after him that seeth me"* (v. 13b). And the wellspring of water at which she sat was henceforth called *Beerlahairoi* (v. 14a). The meaning is unclear, but it likely means either "The well of him that liveth and seeth me," or "the well of the seeing alive," suggesting that Hagar had seen God, yet remained alive.

The primary emphasis of this narrative is not, however, Hagar's sight of God. As amazing as the experience of catching a glimpse of God must have been to her, it was secondary to the superlative reality that God saw her and knew all about the circumstances she faced. How wonderful it is to know the Lord! But the surpassing glory of this thought is even greater: *He sees and knows me, through and through.* Although she was growing in her knowledge of the true and living God, he already knew all about her. God's loving awareness of and personal interest in the lives of his children is always precedent to their knowledge of and familiarity with him (cf. Gal. 4:9a). As an effect to the cause, an experiential knowledge of God is always secondary to God's initiative in grace.

El-Roi Sees Everything

What does this intriguing name for God teach us about his character? The first truth *El-Roi* suggests to our minds is the great fact of the *omniscience* of God. *Omniscience* simply means that God possess all knowledge. He sees and knows everything.

The Psalmist David affirms the all-seeing eye of God in Psalm 11:4: "*The LORD* [Jehovah] *is in his holy temple, the LORD's throne is in heaven: his eyes behold, his eyelids try, the children of men.*" From his heavenly throne, no one and nothing escapes his gaze. In fact, "*all things are naked and open unto him, with whom we have to do*" (Heb. 4:13).

The same thought is reiterated in Psalm 33:13-14: "*The LORD looketh from heaven; he beholdeth all the sons of men. From the place of his habitation he looketh upon all the inhabitants of the earth.*" To this agrees the words of the wise man: "*The eyes of the LORD are in every place, beholding the evil and the good*" (Pro. 15:3). Elihu, also, joins the ranks of those who affirm the omniscience of the Almighty: "*For his eyes are upon the ways of man, and he seeth all his goings*" (Job 34:21). Every thought, intention, desire and deed is open to his penetrating gaze. He sees and knows even the hearts of all men (cf. 2 Sam. 22:28).

El-Roi Sees His People

In an even more particular sense, God watches over his covenant people, looking on them with favor, considering their need, and superintending their lives. Theologians speak of this specific category of God's omniscience in terms of the *providence*[2] of God. The God who sees everything has vouchsafed himself in covenant commitment to oversee the lives of those who belong to him and provide for their needs.

This encouraging truth is stated in Deuteronomy 11, a chapter detailing God's special provision for Israel in the Land of Promise. Speaking of that land and its favored inhabitants, Moses describes it as *"A land which the LORD thy God careth for: the eyes of the LORD thy God are always upon it, from the beginning of the year even unto the end of the year"* (Deut. 11:12). With such an assurance of Jehovah's oversight, the children of Israel could be confident year-round that they were safe in *El-Roi's* care.

The Psalmist, likewise, emphasizes God's providence upon his people. Consider these sublime passages from the Psalter:

- "Behold the eye of the LORD is upon them that fear him, upon them that hope in his mercy; to deliver their soul from death, and to keep them alive in famine" (Ps. 33:18-19)

- "The eyes of the LORD are upon the righteous, and his ears are open unto their cry." (Ps. 34:15)

- "Behold, he that keepeth Israel shall neither slumber nor sleep." (Ps. 121:4)

---

[2] The etymology of the term "providence" (*pro* = pre-, or in advance; *video* = to see) suggests the thought that God "sees in advance," and consequently makes arrangement to satisfy, the needs of his people.

Not only does El-Roi watch over his people with a view toward providing for their needs, he also searches continuously for individuals within his family who need a special manifestation of his grace: "*For the eyes of the LORD run to and fro throughout the whole earth, to show himself strong in the behalf of them whose heart is perfect toward him*" (2 Chr. 16:9a). He notices the submissive and resigned heart and delights to manifest his power in our weakness.

El-Roi Sees Me

But far and away, the most sublime aspect of this Divine name is its personal application. The omniscient God who sees and knows all, especially taking notice of his people, sees me. This profound thought is the theme of Psalm 139.

Notice the spirit of wonder David expresses as he reflects on God's personal knowledge of every aspect of his daily life:

> O LORD, thou hast searched me, and known me. Thou knowest my downsitting and mine uprising, thou understandest my thought afar off. Thou compassest my path and my lying down, and art acquainted with all my ways. For there is not a word in my tongue, but, lo, O LORD, thou knowest it altogether. Thou hast best me behind and before, and laid thine hand upon me. Such knowledge is too wonderful for me; it is high, I cannot attain unto it. (Ps. 139:1-6)

Whatever the circumstances he encounters, David rejoices in the knowledge that God sees him:

> If I say, Surely the darkness shall cover me; even the night shall be light about me. Yea, the darkness hideth not from thee; but the night shineth as the day: the darkness and the light are both alike unto thee. (Ps. 139:11-12)

He then reflects with a profound sense of consolation that God has seen him and watched over his life from his earliest existence, even before he was born into this world:

> For thou hast possessed my reins: thou hast covered me in my mother's womb. I will praise thee; for I am fearfully and wonderfully made: marvelous are thy works; and that my soul knoweth right well. My substance was not hid from thee, when I was made in secret, and curiously wrought in the lowest parts of the earth. Thine eyes did see my substance, yet being unperfect; and in thy book all my members were written, which in continuance were fashioned, when as yet there was none of them. (Ps. 139:13-16)

With such an attentive and loving God watching over every detail of his life, the Psalmist David could live with great confidence for the future...and great vulnerability. Notice the openness he expresses as this Psalm concludes:

> Search me, O God, and know my heart: try me, and know my thoughts: and see if there be any wicked way in me, and lead me in the way everlasting. (Ps. 139:23-24)

I suggest that this kind of vulnerable trust in the God who sees everything there is to see in our lives is the antithesis of our first parents' attempt to hide from God in the Garden (cf. Gen. 3:7-8).

El-Roi, then, is not a name designed for the rich and famous, for kings and queens, celebrities, or the powerful people of the earth. It is a name with special application to common, ordinary people like us—even for simple, lowly and lonely outcasts like Hagar. On this, the worst day of her already dreary and forlorn life, Hagar found comfort in the knowledge that God noticed her.

He also sees and notices you, my friend. Jesus assured his disciples that even the hairs of their heads were all numbered (cf. Mt. 10:30). Is the Father in heaven interested in hair? Not at all, but he is interested in his children, so much so that he sees and knows the minutia of their lives. He sees their every need.

He also sees their afflictions—"*I have seen, I have seen the affliction of my people which is in Egypt,*" the Lord said to Moses, "*and I have heard their groaning, and am come down to deliver them*" (Acts 7:34a; cf. Ex. 3:7)—and their tears: "*Turn again, and tell Hezekiah the captain of my people, Thus saith the LORD, the God of David thy father, I have heard thy prayer, I have seen thy tears: behold I will heal thee...*" (2 Kings 20:5a). He even puts the tears of his people in his bottle of remembrance (cf. Ps. 56:8).

Likewise, *El-Roi* sees when his children are forsaken and forgotten by others. What comfort there is in the thought recorded in Psalm 102:19-20: "*For he hath looked down from the height of his sanctuary; from heaven did the LORD behold the earth; to hear the groaning of the prisoner; to loose those that are appointed to death*"! Just as God saw Hagar's extremity in the desert, so he sees and hears the groaning of the burdened soul from the height of his heavenly throne. When you are tempted, then, to cry with Jonah, "*I am cast out of thy sight*" (Jon. 2:4), let faith remind you of the cheering fact that your God is *El-Roi*, the God who sees his little child when no one else possibly can.

What about those seasons of persecution for righteousness' sake? Does God see me when, as the popular gospel song by the gifted Methodist minister Dr. Charles Tindley (1851-1933) says, "I do the best I can and my friends misunderstand"?[3] Men are only able to behold the outward appearance; consequently, the judgments they make are not always accurate. But God sees the heart and knows the motive behind the action (cf. 1 Sam. 16:7). David, the sweet Psalmist of Israel, took comfort in knowing that when others spoke against him saying, "*Aha, aha, our eye hath seen it,*" God had likewise seen the entire scene and knew the thoughts and intent of his heart: "*This thou hast seen, O LORD*

---

[3] "Stand By Me," Charles Albert Tindley (1905)

[Jehovah]: *keep not silence: O Lord* [Adonai], *be not far from me*" (Ps. 35:21, 22).

Not only does God see the motives of my heart, but he also sees the way I should go. He promises, "*I will instruct thee and teach thee in the way which thou shalt go: I will guide thee with mine eye*" (Ps. 32:8). The name *El-Roi*, then, is the believer's reminder of the reality of Divine guidance. Though we are unable to see beyond the next bend in the road, God observes the whole scene from the exalted vantage point of his heavenly throne, and provides what is needed at each juncture in the journey.

He also sees my secret devotions. Three times in Matthew 6, the Lord Jesus urges his disciples to practice devotional service to God in secret, not in public, like the Pharisees. When prayer, fasting and almsgiving are done with a motive of love to God and others, not with the self-serving aim of proud publicity, God is pleased. And Jesus says, "*Thy Father which seeth in secret himself shall reward thee openly*" (Mt. 6:4, 6, 18). Every act of sincere devotion to him—though unknown, unnoticed and unapplauded by the world—is done in his presence and before his Divine gaze. He is not unrighteous to forget the love you show toward him in each devotional act (cf. Heb. 6:10).

El-Roi Applied

What should we learn from this intriguing, Divine name? First, let it impress upon us the importance of living every moment of our lives *coram Deo*—before the face of God. A conscious awareness that "God sees me," that all of life is lived (as Scripture says) "in his sight,"[4] will have a powerful effect upon the believer's frame of mind and conduct. He sees us at all times and in all places. Nothing escapes his penetrating gaze. When the Christian cultivates the habit of practicing the presence

---

[4] Deuteronomy 6:18; Psalm 19:14; 51:4; Acts 4:19; 2 Corinthians 4:2; 1 Thessalonians 1:3; James 4:10; 1 Peter 3:4; 1 John 3:22

of God (cf. Ps. 16:8)—aware that he is *El-Roi*—every part of life will be dramatically impacted.

Secondly, let this name strengthen and comfort you in your moments of trial and difficulty. Are you lost, confused and forlorn, like Hagar? Do you face joblessness, conflict in marriage, or mistreatment? Do you live with a physical disability or impairment? Is your heart broken with grief? He sees and knows. *El-Roi* notices your plight and cares for your distress. And he will come to help and deliver you, just as surely as he delivered the poor Egyptian outcast. May you, today, see the God who seeth you.

8
El-Elyon: **The Most High God**

"There is a river, the streams whereof shall make glad the city of God, the holy place of the tabernacles of the most High." Psalm 46:4

The Hebrew name *El-Elyon*, translated "the most High God," occurs 28 times in the Old Testament, nineteen of which are in the Psalms. It first appears in Genesis 14:18-22, the narrative of Abram's encounter with the mysterious character named Melchizedek as he returned from battling the kings of the valley and rescuing his nephew Lot. Melchizedek is called the *"priest of the most high God* [El-Elyon]*"* (Gen. 14:18), even before the Levitical priesthood was established under the Mosaic covenant. As such, Melchizedek prefigures the Lord Jesus Christ, our everlasting High Priest (cf. Heb. 7:1-17).

When Abram gave one-tenth of the spoils he took in battle unto Melchizedek, he demonstrated by that action his understanding of Melchizedek's superiority to him. In return, Melchizedek pronounced a benediction upon Abram, saying, *"Blessed be Abram of the most high God* [El-Elyon], *possessor of heaven and earth: and blessed be the most high God* [El-Elyon], *which hath delivered thine enemies into thy hand"* (Gen. 14:19-20).

Subsequently, when the king of Sodom offered Abram the remaining spoils as payment for his services, Abram swore an oath before the him saying, *"I have lift up mine hand unto the LORD* [Jehovah], *the most high God* [El-Elyon], *the possessor of heaven and earth, that I will not take from a thread even to a shoelatchet, and that I will not take any thing that is thine, lest thou shouldest say, I have made Abram rich..."* (14:22-23).

At least two important thoughts may be gleaned from the initial occurrence of this Divine name. First, it is clear from verse 22 that *El-Elyon* and *Jehovah* are one and the same. *El-Elyon* is simply another manifestation of the character of God. Secondly, *El-Elyon* is *"the possessor of heaven and earth"* (vs. 19, 22). He owns it all by right of creation (cf. Ps. 24:1).

Note also that this term is a superlative. The "most High" suggests the idea of a *hierarchy*.[1] *El-Elyon* occupies the position of highest rank in this universe. He is "the highest of the high." He is "the God of gods" (Ps. 136:2), "the King of kings and Lord of lords" (1 Tim. 6:15), a formula designed to describe the ultimate or superlative degree. Ecclesiastes 5:8 expresses this thought: *"If thou seest the oppression of the poor, and violent perverting of judgment and justice in a province, marvel not at the matter: for he that is higher than the highest regardeth; and there be higher than they."* *El-Elyon*, then, is the final authority, the ultimate ruler and king who observes every detail of human affairs and metes out justice and judgment even when earthly leaders fail to hold criminals to account.

Elyon is also the designation preferred by the angel Gabriel. In the universal hierarchy, angels are beneath the Father and the Son, man is a little lower than the angels, and animals are beneath man (cf. Heb. 1:4ff; Ps. 8:5-8; Heb. 2:5-9). The angel Gabriel, consequently—unlike the arch-angel Lucifer who aspired to *"be like the most High* [Elyon]" (Is. 14:12-14)—is quick to acknowledge that none are higher than God.

Gabriel announced the immaculate conception to Mary in these terms: *"He shall be great, and shall be called the Son of the Highest* [Elyon]: *and the Lord God shall give unto him the throne of his father David…"* (Lk. 1:32). When Mary asked how this might occur seeing she had not known a man, Gabriel replied, *"The Holy Ghost shall come upon thee, and the power of the Highest* [Elyon] *shall overshadow thee…"* (Lk. 1:35). Zacharias also employed the term in his benediction upon his own preborn son, John the Baptist: *"And thou, child, shalt be called the*

---

[1] A hierarchy is an arrangement of items in order of rank or authority.

prophet of the Highest [Elyon]: *for thou shalt go before the face of the Lord to prepare his ways*" (Lk. 1:76).

Our God, then, is "His Highness." The entire angelic host, not just Gabriel, celebrates him as such: "*I have commanded my sanctified ones, I have also called my mighty ones for mine anger, even them that rejoice in my highness*" (Is. 13:3). Of all the high positions among men, *Jehovah* is "*the most high over all the earth*" (Ps. 83:18). Let's be a bit more specific now concerning the significance of this name. We will ask two questions: (1) First, what does *El-Elyon* mean? (2) Secondly, what does *El-Elyon* mean to us?

Doctrine: What Does *El-Elyon* Mean?

The name *El-Elyon* conveys the thought of twin, Divine attributes. Theologians speak of these in terms of the Supremacy, or Majesty, of God, and the Sovereignty of God.

Here is a helpful criterion for measuring truth. Truth will always exalt the glory of God and abase the pride of man. No other Divine name stresses this high view of God like the name *El-Elyon*. Consider, as a case in point, Isaiah 33:5: "*The LORD is exalted; for he dwelleth on high: he hath filled Zion with judgment and righteousness.*" The New Testament, likewise, maintains this exalted language in connection with the Lord Jesus Christ: "*…and of whom as concerning the flesh Christ came, who is over all, God blessed for ever. Amen*" (Rom. 9:5); "*For there is no difference between the Jew and the Greek: for the same Lord over all is rich unto all that call upon him*" (Rom. 10:12). Over and again, Bible writers remind us that the Lord is exalted on high; consequently, he rules and reigns over all.

It is for this reason that he is called "*the high and lofty One that inhabiteth eternity*" (Is. 57:15a) and "*the Highest*" (Ps. 18:13; 87:5), and is said to dwell "in the high and holy place" (cf. Is. 57:15b). Psalm 113:4-8 is a veritable anthem to the absolute supremacy and majesty of God:

The LORD is high above all nations, and his glory above the
   heavens.
Who is like unto the LORD our God, who dwelleth on high,
Who humbleth himself to behold the things that are in heaven,
   and in the earth!
He raiseth up the poor out of the dust, and lifteth the needy out
   of the dunghill;
That he may set him with princes, even with the princes of his
   people.

What are the implications of this high, transcendent view of
God? To say that God is supreme means that

- He is higher than his own creation (Is. 40:26; Acts 7:48;
  17:24)[2]
- He is higher than the idols of men (Ps. 95:3; 96:4; 97:9)
- He is higher than his people (Ps. 99:2-3, 5)
- He is higher than earthly kings and potentates (Ps. 89:27)
- He is higher than the heavens (Heb. 7:26; Is. 52:13; Acts
  5:31; Phi. 2:9)
- His ways and thoughts are higher than man's ways and
  thoughts, just as the heavens are higher than the earth (cf.
  Is. 55:9)
- He is exalted as head above all (1 Chr. 29:11).

This name, furthermore, teaches a doctrine known as the
sovereignty of God. Divine sovereignty means that God has
absolute, unchallenged authority. The account of
Nebuchadnezzar's pride, subsequent insanity and transformation
is the classic illustration of God's sovereignty over all. In the
disclosure of his dream, Nebuchadnezzar details the sentence of

---

[2] Pantheism, the worldview expressed by mystical religions like Buddhism and
Hinduism, teaches that there is no distinction between God and the world that
he made.

judgment he heard (cf. Dan. 4:16) and the purpose of the sentence:

"...To the intent that the living may know that the most High [*Elyon*] ruleth in the kingdom of men, and giveth it to whomsoever he will, and setteth up over it the basest of men" (Dan. 4:17b).

What was the purpose of God's judgment upon Nebuchadnezzar? It was intended to teach him that he was not the ultimate authority—that he did not reign without accountability to One who was even higher than he.

The narrative of Daniel 4 proceeds to record the execution of the sentence on the king of Babylon. One year after the dream, the proud king surveyed his kingdom with self-admiration, saying, *"Is not this great Babylon, that I have built for the house of the kingdom by the might of my power, and for the honor of my majesty?"* (Dan. 4:30). While the word was in his mouth, Divine judgment fell on Nebuchadnezzar. His reason—lit. capacity to think rationally—was taken from him and he was compelled to vacate his throne. The king relocated to the pasture to live with the beasts of the field.

For the next seven years,[3] Nebuchadnezzar grazed on grass like the oxen, remained outside throughout night so that his body was wet with the dew of heaven, and failed to maintain personal hygiene, so that his hair assumed the appearance of eagle's

---

[3] The reference to "seven times" in Daniel 4 is, as Calvin stated, "naturally indefinite." If one assumes on the basis of the expression "a time, times and a half" (cf. Dan. 12:7) that a "time" in Daniel is equivalent to one year, then it is reasonable to conclude that Nebuchadnezzar's insanity lasted for seven years. The word may refer, however, to "seasons," in which case the period labeled "seven times" may be closer to three and one-half years, alternating the transition from summer to winter seven times. Other scholastics assume the time-frame may refer to seven months, or even seven weeks. Since there is no consensus among Bible students, it seems to me that using the model indigenous to the prophecy of the book of Daniel, i.e. one time equals one year, is the safest explanation.

feathers and his nails grew like the claws of a bird. The insane king of Babylon must have been a spectacle to both his own subjects and every foreign dignitary that visited the palace.

When the days of judgment were finished, Nebuchadnezzar's sanity was restored. With the return of his reason came a completely new worldview. He sang a different tune than before his humiliation:

> "And at the end of the days I Nebuchadnezzar lifted up mine eyes unto heaven, and mine understanding returned unto me, and I blessed the most High [*Elyon*], and I praised and honored him that liveth for ever, whose dominion is an everlasting dominion, and his kingdom is from generation to generation: and all the inhabitants of the earth are reputed as nothing: and he doeth according to his will in the army of heaven, and among the inhabitants of the earth: and none can stay his hand, or say unto him, What doest thou?" (Dan. 4:34-35).

There is arguably no better definition of the sovereignty of God than this. The most High God does according to his will in heaven and earth; no man nor devil can hinder his work, nor does anyone have the right to question him.

It sounds as if God is doing what he pleases, doesn't it. Asking no permission and seeking no advice, he occupies the position of ultimate authority in the universe. The buck stops here.

To say that God is sovereign is simply to say that God is God. Beside him there is no other; therefore, he does what he pleases, when he pleases, how he pleases, where he pleases, and to whom he pleases, and no man has the ability to stay his hand or right to object to his decisions. *"Our God is in the heavens: he hath done whatsoever he hath pleased"* (Ps. 115:3).

Later, when Nebuchadnezzar's son Belshazzar reigned as king, Daniel the prophet was again summoned to interpret the king's dream. Daniel began by rehearsing the fact that *"the most high God* [El-Elyon] *gave Nebuchadnezzar thy father a kingdom, and majesty, and glory, and honor: and for the majesty that he gave him, all people, nations, and languages, trembled and feared before him...*" (Dan. 5:18-19).

Notice that Daniel ascribes Nebuchadnezzar's political power and influence to God, not to the king's own prowess or skill. Then he recounts how Nebuchadnezzar was lifted up in pride, humbled by God's judgment, and repented, confessing that "*the most high God* [El-Elyon] *rule(s) in the kingdom of men, and that he appointeth over it whomsoever he will*" (Dan. 5:20-21). Then Daniel confronts Belshazzar for refusing to humble himself before the Sovereign God of heaven and earth, announcing his imminent defeat (cf. 5:22-29). That very night, Belshazzar was slain.

A sovereign possesses plenipotentiary[4], or autonomous, power. He is a law unto himself, invested with the authority to act unilaterally. The God of heaven is, of course, the only true sovereign, for he is the ultimate authority: "*When the most High* [Elyon] *divided to the nations their inheritance, when he separated the sons of Adam, he set the bounds of the people according to the number of the children of Israel. For the LORD's portion is his people; Jacob is the lot of his inheritance*" (Deut. 32:8-9).

The 47th Psalm is a rhapsody to the unchallenged authority and invincible power of *El-Elyon*:

> O clap your hands, all ye people; shout unto God with the voice of triumph.
> For the LORD most high [*Jehovah Elyon*] is terrible; he is a great King over all the earth...
> Sing praises to God, sing praises: sing praises unto our King, sing praises.
> For God is the King of all the earth: sing ye praises with understanding.

---

[4] The term derives from two Latin words: *plenus* meaning "full," and *potens* meaning "power." Plenipotentiary power, then, is full, absolute authority.

God reigneth over the heathen: God sitteth upon the throne of his
holiness..." (vs. 1-2, 6-8)

Such a high view of God is tremendously important for the
Christian. Sadly, many have heard for so long about a God who
wants to save sinners but, because of man's refusal to cooperate,
is frustrated and defeated. The biblical portrait of the Deity,
however, is not one of a thwarted, foiled, hand-wringing, floor-
pacing God who can't unless sinful mortals let him. Rather, the
sovereign Ruler of heaven and earth "*is in one mind, and who
can turn him? And what his soul desireth, even that he doeth*"
(Job 23:13). When he speaks, it is done; when he commands, it
stands fast (Ps. 33:9).

Because he is the most High, *El-Elyon* is not handcuffed by
man's resistance; his sovereign will is not a victim of the sinner's
obstinate will: "*Remember the former things of old: for I am God,
and there is none else; I am God, and there is none like me,
declaring the end from the beginning, and from ancient times the
things that are not yet done, saying, My counsel shall stand, and I
will do all my pleasure...I have spoken it, I will also bring it to
pass; I have purposed it, I will also do it*" (Is. 46:9-10, 11b).
When he works, none can hinder; when he hinders, none can
work (cf. Is. 43:13).

So many professing believers today need to take a trip down to
the potter's house for the purpose of observing a potter at work
on a piece of clay (cf. Jer. 18). For so long, they've been taught
that man's will is sovereign—that the sinner makes the
determinative choice—and that God is essentially limited in what
he can do by man's decision. Just a few minutes observing a
potter molding clay into a vessel of his own prerogative,
however, may prove very instructive of this fundamental
principle, namely, that God may deal with man in the same way
the potter deals with a lump of clay.

Romans chapters nine, ten and eleven form a theodicy, or
justification of God, in terms of his righteousness in dealing with

the nation of Israel. The first argument Paul presents to vindicate God concerns the sovereignty of God (Romans 9). And the example he selects to illustrate Divine sovereignty is his decree of election (Rom. 9:11ff). The apostle establishes in no uncertain terms that God made choice of Jacob while bypassing Esau by virtue of his own right to do as he pleases. He asks, *"What shall we say then? Is there unrighteousness with God?"* And he answers, *"God forbid,"* for the Potter has authority to make from the clay whatever he purposes to make.

It is clear from this chapter that the tension people feel about the doctrine of election is not with the doctrine itself, but with the sovereignty of God. The natural man would rather God be anywhere but on his throne. The believer, on the contrary, understands that if God had not acted to choose a people from the fallen lump of humanity as his own, none would be saved, for depraved sinners are so averse and antagonistic toward God that they would never, apart from Divine grace, choose him.

The exalted view of God expressed by this Divine name, *El-Elyon* (the most High God), then, is basic and fundamental to an accurate understanding of God's character. It is also personally relevant to our lives now.

Application: What Does *El-Elyon* Mean to Us?

The recovery of the important truth of Divine sovereignty is vitally important to the spiritual health of individual believers as well as the church at a corporate level. It is essential because, as contemporary theologian and bible teacher J. I. Packer says, we are living in "the age of the God-shrinkers" in which we have "unwarrantably great thoughts of humanity and scandalously small thoughts of God."[5] Modern man looks at God through the wrong end of the telescope, making him appear much smaller than he really is, then turns the contraption around to look at

---

[5] Packer, *Rediscovering Holiness* (Servant Publications, 1992), p. 68.

himself, concluding that he is greater and more important than he actually is.

We are impressed by celebrities and athletes, presidents and popes, eager to rub shoulders with the rich and famous, but bored with a God-centered sermon or book on theology. Man seems so much more real to us fallen sinners—and interesting—than the God of heaven and earth. Is our moral and theological nearsightedness not the equivalent of idolatry? By elevating ourselves and our fellow mortals to the position of priority above God, we repeat the sin of Lucifer who aspired "to be like *Elyon*" (cf. Is. 14:14). Every man-made religion, as a matter of fact— whether atheism, polytheism, humanism, statism, animism, or pantheism[6]—is a violation of the first commandment, the Divine prohibition against idolatry (cf. Ex. 20:3), and a challenge to God as *El-Elyon*, the ultimate Authority. What an outrageous act and reversal of the Divine hierarchy it is, then, for someone to elevate an animal to a level of devotion and worship above "the most High God"! Is it any wonder that God would respond to such a monstrous perversion of the created order by withdrawing his governing influence from such a culture (cf. Rom. 1:21-32)?

I am confident that the need to see God "high and lifted up" (cf. Is. 6:1ff) has never been greater than it is in our post-modern world. What will be the benefit of such a high view of the sovereign God of heaven and earth? It will impact us in at least three distinct ways.

First, the awareness that he is *El-Elyon*, the most High God, will prove our **incentive to exalt and glorify him in all that we do.** Worship is essentially an act of exalting and glorifying the

---

[6] Atheism denies the existence of God. Polytheism, or the worship of a multiplicity of gods, puts imagination in God's place. Humanism, or the deification of mankind, transposes man to the place of God. Statism, or emperor worship, puts the government in the place of God. Animism, or nature worship, ascribes a soul or spiritual essence to animals, plants and even inanimate objects in nature. Pantheism, as expressed in the mystical religions, depersonalizes God into an energy, force or spirit present in every physical reality.

Lord, for he alone is worthy. The greater is our grasp of his transcendent greatness and majesty, the greater will be our worship: *"Great is the Lord and greatly to be praised..."* (Ps. 48:1a). Hence, David expresses his desire to see God exalted and glorified: *"Be thou exalted, O God, above the heavens: let thy glory be above all the earth"* (Ps. 57:11). In so doing, he aligns himself with God's own self-regard for the glory of his own name: *"Be still and know that I am God: I will be exalted among the heathen, I will be exalted in the earth"* (Ps. 46:10).

Of course, man cannot exalt the Lord in the sense of making him any higher or greater than he already is. But we can confess and acknowledge him as "high and lifted up." We can celebrate his exalted glory and position of honor. Men can "ascribe greatness" to the Lord (cf. Deut. 32:3b). Isaiah 12:4 puts it as follows: *"And in that day shall ye say, Praise the LORD, call upon his name, declare his doings among the people, make mention that his name is exalted."* And Psalm 18:46 describes it like this: *"The LORD liveth; and blessed be my rock; and let the God of my salvation be exalted."* That is the language of worship.

But exalting the highest God involves more than the act of worshipping and praising him. We also honor his highness by refusing to challenge his sovereign authority—by bowing humbly and obediently in submission to the authority of his word. In the wilderness, the Israelites incurred God's displeasure and judgment because they challenged his authority: *"Yet they tempted and provoked the most high God* [El-Elyon]*, and kept not his testimonies"* (Ps. 78:56). Bondage and captivity typically await the individual (or nation) that rebels *"against the words of God"* and condemns *"the counsel of the most High"* [Elyon] (Ps. 107:10-11). Acknowledging that the most high God possesses authority over every area of our lives—whether our faith, conduct, thought patterns, attitudes, decisions, relationships or money—by means of obeying his word is a response to this Divine attribute as crucial as the act of worship.

Secondly, knowing God as *El-Elyon* is our **incentive to trust him, for he is in ultimate control of the world he made and the circumstances of our lives**. I find great comfort in the knowledge that God is not only greater than the storms of life, but the frightening noise of those storms:

> The floods have lifted up, O LORD, the floods have lifted up their voice; the floods lift up their waves. The LORD on high is mightier than the noise of many waters, yea, than the mighty waves of the sea. (Ps. 93:3-4)

Like a small child shrinks in fear at the sound of crashing thunder, or like a sudden loud noise strikes unsuspecting bystanders with panic, people are not immune to the fear of perceived danger. Ask the parent of a prodigal child about the effect a ringing telephone has on his/her emotional state. Ask an employee of a downsizing company who has just received notice that he has been summoned to the boss's office. Even when the fear is realized, however, the sovereign Lord is still in control. Looking back on the experience at some point in the future may very well prove that the thing you were so afraid of was little more than just "noise." As difficult as the trial may seem at the moment, it is no match for *El-Elyon*. As high as the waves of trouble may swell, our God is higher still.

In times of distress, Old Testament saints turned instinctively to this name. Consider these examples from the Psalms:

- From the end of the earth will I cry unto thee, when my heart is overwhelmed: lead me to the rock that is higher [*elyon*] than I. – Psalm 61:2
- He that dwelleth in the secret place of the most High [*Elyon*] shall abide under the shadow of the Almighty [*Shaddai*]. – Psalm 91:1

- Because thou has made the LORD [*Jehovah*], which is my refuge, even the most High [*Elyon*], thy habitation... - Psalm 91:9
- It is a good thing to give thanks unto the LORD [*Jehovah*], and to sing praises unto thy name, O most High [*Elyon*]... - Psalm 92:1
- When the wicked spring as the grass, and when all the workers of iniquity do flourish; it is that they shall be destroyed forever: but thou, LORD [*Jehovah*], art most high [*elyon*] for evermore. – Psalm 92:7-8

When storms of affliction strike, still *"There is a river, the streams whereof shall make glad the city of God, the holy place of the tabernacles of the most High* [Elyon]" (Ps. 46:4). In times of persecution, we may appeal to One who is above this earthly fray—*"Mine enemies would daily swallow me up: for they be many that fight against me, O thou most High* [Elyon]. *What time I am afraid, I will trust in thee"* (Ps. 56:2-3)—and trust him to work on our behalf: *"I will cry unto God most high* [El-Elyon]; *unto God that performeth all things for me"* (Ps. 57:2).

When David fled for safety at the news of Absalom's insurrection, the rightful king found solace in a King even higher than he: *"I will be glad and rejoice in thee: I will sing praise to thy name, O thou most High* [Elyon]. *When mine enemies are turned back, they shall fall and perish at thy presence. For thou hast maintained my right and my cause; thou satest in the throne judging right"* (Ps. 9:2-4). And when it seems as if God has hidden his smiling face, the believer may reflect on the past displays of his sovereign God as reason to hope for restoration in the future: *"Hath God forgotten to be gracious? Hath he in anger shut up his tender mercies? Selah. And I said, This is my infirmity: but I will remember the years of the right hand of the most High* [Elyon]" (Ps. 77:9-10).

The story of the three Hebrew children, described by the Babylonian king as *"servants of the most high God"* [El-Elyon], reminds us of the fact that God takes care of his faithful servants. In fact, His Highness, the exalted One, "*sets them on high after affliction*" (Ps. 107:41) and exalts them to their own "*high places*" (Ps. 18:33). The ultimate "high place" in this present realm is the exalted privilege of entering into the blessed experience of life in the Lord's kingdom, a blessing that will continue even into the eternal state: "*But the saints of the most High* [Elyon] *shall take the kingdom, and possess the kingdom for ever, even for ever and ever*" (Dan. 7:18; cf. 7:22-27). Come what may, *El-Elyon* abundantly compensates his true servants; therefore, we trust him to exalt us.

Finally, an understanding of the significance of this magnificent name serves as our **incentive to anticipate the day when he alone is exalted**. Isaiah 2:11-18 contains promise of a future day in which the pride of man, together with all his idols, will be demolished and the Lord alone exalted. Notice the contrast between all that is "lofty" in this world and God's supremacy:

> ...For the day of the LORD of hosts shall be upon every one that is proud and lofty...and upon all the cedars of Lebanon, that are high and lifted up, and upon all the oaks of Bashan, and upon all the high mountains, and upon all the hills that are lifted up, and upon every high tower, and upon every fenced wall, and upon all the ships of Tarshish, and upon all pleasant pictures. And the loftiness of man shall be bowed down, and the haughtiness of men shall be made low: and the LORD alone shall be exalted in that day. And the idols he shall utterly abolish.

How thrilling will be that day when every earthly monarch will abandon his throne—when every high thing that exalts itself against the Lord and against his Christ; when every proud look from arrogant sinners dissolves in fear that the God so long despised and defied now holds them to an account; when every knee will bow and every tongue confess that Jesus Christ is Lord, the only Potentate, King of kings and Lord of lords! Then every blasphemous and proud mouth will be silenced. Then all the hard speeches that ungodly sinners have spoken against him will be forever muted, for *El-Elyon*, the most High God, comes to judge the world in righteousness. No wonder the saints who long for the glory and honor of his name will sing, *"Alleluia, for the Lord God omnipotent reigneth!"* (Rev. 19:4).

9
El-Olam: The Everlasting God

"Hast thou not known? Hast thou not heard? That the everlasting God, the LORD, the Creator of the ends of the earth fainteth not; neither is weary? (Isaiah 40:28)

The Hebrew word *olam*, translated in the King James Translation by the terms *everlasting*, *eternal*, and *forever*, means "the vanishing point; time unmeasured; ageless." It suggests the thought of something beyond the horizon, which is the limit of human vision and the point at which sensory perception vanishes.

Olam can either point backward, to the remote past, as it does in Psalm 25:6,[1] or forward, to the distant future, as it does in Psalm 100:5.[2] Periodically, a verse contains the term to point in both directions, as it does in Psalme 103:17: *"But the mercy of the LORD is from everlasting [olam] to everlasting [olam] upon them that fear him, and his righteousness unto children's children"* (Ps. 103:17). The majority of references to *olam* in the Old Testament, consequently, suggest the idea of something which is "endless in duration; perpetual; never-ending."

When attached to the name of God, *olam* speaks of the enduring quality of all God's ways and works. It adds a further nuance to the primary name *Jehovah*. As we have seen, *Jehovah*[3] reveals God as the eternally present, self-existent God who possesses the power of being within himself; hence, it essentially starts from where we are and looks backward to the One who is the First Cause and origin of existence. *Olam*, on the other hand,

---

[1] *"Remember, O LORD, thy tender mercies and lovingkindnesses; for they have been ever of old."*

[2] *"For the LORD is good; his mercy everlasting; and his truth endureth to all generations."*

[3] *Jehovah*, scholastically termed the *tetragrammaton*, derives from the expression *"I am that I am"* in Exodus 3:14.

adds a definite reference to the future, depicting God as one who is endless and whose Divine purpose will be finally realized; hence, it essentially starts from where we are and looks forward to the ultimate outcome.

El-Olam, translated by the expression "Everlasting God," speaks of him as the "God of the ages," or the "God of generations." The theological truth on display in this particular name is the attribute of God's *eternality*. To say that God is eternal is to say that he is without beginning and without end. Consider the following references to the eternality of God:

- The eternal God [*El-Olam*] is thy refuge, and underneath are the everlasting arms... (Deut. 33:27a)
- Before the mountains were brought forth, or ever thou hadst formed the earth and the world, even from everlasting [*olam*] to everlasting [*olam*], thou art God. (Ps. 90:2)
- Thy throne is established of old: thou art from everlasting [*olam*]. (Ps. 93:2)
- But thou, Bethlehem Ephratah, though thou be little among the thousands of Judah, yet out of thee shall he come forth unto me that is to be ruler in Israel; whose goings forth have been from of old, from everlasting [*olam*]. (Mic. 5:2)
- Art thou not from everlasting [*olam*], O LORD my God, mine Holy One? (Hab. 1:12a)

The first occurrence of this name is Genesis 21:33: "*And Abraham planted a grove in Beersheba, and called there on the name of the LORD, the everlasting God* [El-Olam]." The point intended by that initial Biblical reference to this name is clear: the God of Abraham is timeless. He is, as the Pauline doxology in 1 Timothy 1:17 states, "*the King eternal*," which literally means "King of the ages." Though times and circumstances change, *El-Olam* does not. He is the same in all ages, seasons, and conditions. Let's explore two particular areas of significance related to this Divine name.

God's Attributes are *Olam*

The text that heads this chapter assures God's people that the "everlasting God," by virtue of the fact of his eternal nature, is immutable.[4] He is not subject to variation in circumstance or environment, or subject to any external influence or stimuli. Nothing victimizes or influences God, else he would not (and could not) be eternal.

Of course, human beings are not eternal. That is evident by the fact that people change. Our health changes; energy waxes and wanes. We age. We change our minds. Emotions rise and fall. Memory lapses. Ambition fades. At the zenith of his life, man performs at the top of his game. But the glory of man is short-lived. It fades and wilts like a beautiful flower (cf. Is. 40:6). It is not long before he is a mere shadow of his former self.

But God never changes. He cannot change for the better, for he is already infinite, nor for the worse, for he is essentially holy. He never ages, grows weary, tired, or fatigued. The everlasting God *"fainteth not, neither is weary"* (Is. 40:28). The passage of time has not diminished either his ability to hear the prayers of his children or to deliver them in the battles they fight: *"The LORD's hand is not shortened, that it cannot save; neither his ear heavy, that it cannot hear"* (Is. 59:1). What a comfort it is to know that *"He that keepeth thee will not slumber. Behold, he that keepeth Israel shall neither slumber nor sleep"* (Ps. 121:3b-4)!

The **power of our everlasting God is eternal** (cf. Rom. 1:20); hence, we may sing the popular children's hymn, "The God who lived in the olden times, is just the same today." His **love is eternal**. The God who affirmed his covenant loyalty to Israel saying, *"I have loved thee with an everlasting [olam] love; therefore with lovingkindness have I drawn thee"* (Jer. 31:3), has also promised all of his people that absolutely nothing can

---

[4] *Immutable* means "without mutation, or change." God is unchangeable (cf. Jas. 1:17; Mal. 3:6; Heb. 13:8).

separate them from the love of God that is in Christ Jesus (cf. Rom. 8:35ff).

Likewise his **goodness is eternal**. *El Olam* is endlessly benevolent: "*...the goodness of God endureth continually*" (Ps. 52:1b). And so is **his mercy eternal**. Psalm 136 is an anthem to the everlasting mercy of God. Every one of its twenty-six verses ends with the celebratory refrain, "*for his mercy endureth for ever.*"

In the previous chapter, we considered the fact that God is sovereign. When we consider this name, *El-Olam*, as yet a further revelation of the character of God, we discover that he is even **eternal in his sovereign reign**. *El-Elyon*, the most high God, is also *El-Olam*, the everlasting God—everlasting, that is, even in his sovereignty.

The transformed king of Babylon observed this much when he confessed, that "*the most High* [Elyon]*...liveth for ever, whose dominion is an everlasting* [olam] *dominion, and his kingdom is from generation to generation*" (Dan. 4:34). Psalm 45:6 agrees: "*Thy throne,[5] O God, is for ever and ever: the sceptre of thy kingdom is a right sceptre.*"

God's Actions are *Olam*

Not only does this Hebrew name teach us that God's attributes are eternal, but it also assures us that his actions are likewise everlasting. The wise man wrote, "*I know that whatsoever God doeth, it shall be for ever: nothing can be put to it, nor any thing taken from it: and God doeth it that men should fear before him*" (Ecc. 3:14).

First, **his covenant purpose is eternal**. Ephesians 3:11 speaks of God's "*eternal purpose which he purposed in Christ Jesus our Lord.*" *El-Olam* is the God who has pledged himself to keep covenant by implementing every detail until the plan culminates

---

[5] Scriptural references to God's "throne" remind us of the theological truth of Divine sovereignty. A king is, by definition, sovereign.

at his designed goal: *"Which in his times he shall show, who is the blessed and only Potentate, the King of kings, and Lord of lords"* (1 Tim. 6:15). His covenant decree is termed *"the commandment of the everlasting God"* in Romans 16:26, and the covenant of redemption itself is called *"the everlasting covenant"* in Hebrews 13:20. The very language affirms the immutability and certainty of the covenant of grace.

Secondly, the grace of **imputed righteousness is everlasting**. The prophecy of Daniel 9:24 indicates that Messiah would procure on behalf of his people an everlasting righteousness: *"Seventy weeks are determined upon thy people and upon thy holy city, to finish the transgression, to make an end of sins, and to make reconciliation for iniquity, and to bring in everlasting [olam] righteousness..."* The Savior's act of substitution and imputation in place of God's elect is a permanent, immutable work.

Further, **his priestly office is eternal**: *"But this man, because he continueth ever, hath an unchangeable priesthood"* (Heb. 7:24). The High Priest that made the one offering for sin forever now intercedes at the right hand of God on behalf of those for whom he made sacrifice. His session in the very presence of God guarantees that those he redeemed will receive every benefit of his atoning sacrifice on their behalf.

In a word, **the gift of salvation**, in all of its parts and details, **is eternal**. Both the Lord Jesus and the apostle Paul refer to the gift of salvation in terms of "eternal life." In the real "Lord's Prayer," John chapter seventeen, our Lord prays for the Father's endorsement on the work of redemption: *"As thou hast given [thy Son] power over all flesh, that he should give eternal life to as many as thou hast given him. And this is life eternal, that they might know thee the only true God, and Jesus Christ, whom thou hast sent"* (Jno. 17:2-3). And Paul, writing to Titus, defines "the faith of God's elect" in terms of the hope of eternal life: *"In hope of eternal life, which God, that cannot lie, promised before the world began"* (Titus 1:2). Again, in Hebrews 9:12, he insists that

Jesus Christ, our Great High Priest, *"entered in once into the holy place, having obtained eternal redemption for us."*

These references affirm that eternal salvation began in the covenant of redemption before the foundation of the world, a covenant in which the Father, that cannot lie, gave a people to his Son (here is election); that the Son went to the cross on behalf of these very people and procured redemption for them (here is particular redemption); and that the Son, subsequently, gives eternal life as a gift of grace to that very people by working within their hearts to bring them to a relational knowledge of the Father and the Son (here is regeneration). Because the gift of salvation from sin is eternal, it can never be forfeited or lost (here is preservation in grace). To his covenant people God says, *"Can a woman forget her sucking child that she should not have compassion on the son of her womb? Yea, they may forget, yet will I not forget thee. Behold, I have graven thee upon the palms of my hands; thy walls are continually before me"* (Is. 49:15-16).

"Walls" suggest the image of protecting a city. In this reassuring promise, God pledges to be the Heavenly Watchman, ever vigilant to protect his children from whatever may threaten their souls. Shifting metaphors, the passage further affirms that the spiritual union that exists between him and his covenant people is as permanent as if they were engraved as an organic part of his own body. And the fact that their names are graven upon the palms of his hands indicates that he is perpetually reminded of them, just as the person who writes a note on his palm is reminded of it on each occasion in which he lifts his hand before his eyes. He will never forget his own.

This doctrine of the eternal security of the saints means that they have a heavenly inheritance that is kept for them and they for it (cf. 1 Pet. 1:4-5). It is "a better and an enduring substance"—better because it, unlike the corruptible possessions a person may accumulate in this world, endures (cf. Heb. 10:34).

In the fifth place, *the bliss* that awaits the people so blessed by *El-Olam*, the everlasting God, *will be eternal*, just as the punishment of the wicked will never end. Consider these Bible references to the everlasting character of both the joy of the righteous and the judgment of the wicked:

- For we know that if our earthly house of this tabernacle were dissolved, we have a building of God, an house not made with hands, eternal in the heavens. (2 Cor. 5:1)
- For here we have no continuing city, but we seek one to come. (Heb. 13:14)
- But the God of all grace who hath called us unto his eternal glory by Christ Jesus... (1 Pet. 5:10a)
- And these shall go away into everlasting punishment: but the righteous into life eternal. (Mt. 25:46)
- And many of them that sleep in the dust of the earth shall awake, some to everlasting life, and some to shame and everlasting contempt. (Dan. 12:2)
- Who shall be punished with everlasting destruction from the presence of the Lord, and from the presence of the Lord, and from the glory of his power. (2 Ths. 1:9)
- O thou enemy, destructions are come to *a perpetual end...* (Ps. 9:6a – emphasis added)

Scripture further teaches that his kingdom will last forever (cf. Dan. 2:44; 2 Pet. 1:11; Eph. 3:21), and the gospel, i.e. good news, of that kingdom is, likewise, everlasting (Rev. 14:6; Mt. 24:35; Is. 40:8). Because our God is *El-Olam*, God everlasting, the promise of his abiding presence is perennially and perpetually pertinent: "...*and lo, I am with you always, even unto the end of the world. Amen*" (Mt. 28:20b).

PART 3

COMPOUNDS OF *JEHOVAH*

10
Jehovah-Jireh: The Lord will Provide

"And Abraham called the name of that place Jehovah-jireh: as it is said to this day, In the mount of the LORD it shall be seen." (Genesis 22:14)

We move now to consider several of the compounds of the name *Jehovah*, the personal name for God. *Jehovah*, as noted in chapter 3, is the God of grace who has entered into covenant relationship with his people. It is his relational name. Each of the compounds attached to this name, subsequently, serve to amplify that quality of personal relationship by revealing specific areas in which the covenant relationship manifests itself.

These compound names are generally revealed in connection with some specific episode in the history of God's people. The purpose is to portray Jehovah in a particular aspect of his character that meets human need.

The first of the compound names of *Jehovah*, and possibly the most well-known, is *Jehovah-Jireh*, a combination of terms which likely means, *the LORD will provide*. It derives from a single narrative in the Old Testament, i.e. the story of Abraham and Isaac on Mount Moriah, recorded in Genesis 22. We will approach the narrative and meaning of this profoundly sublime name by considering, first, the historical details, next, the geographical setting, and finally, the theological significance.

The Historical Details

Genesis 22 contains three main points. First, it demonstrates Abraham's faith and obedience in a time of Divine testing. Secondly, it depicts Isaac's willing submission to his father. Thirdly, it displays Jehovah's provision of a substitute.

The chapter begins with a startling Divine commission to Abraham: "*And it came to pass after these things, that God did tempt Abraham, and said unto him, Abraham: and he said,*

Behold, here I am. And he said, Take now thy son, thine only son Isaac, whom thou lovest, and get thee into the land of Moriah; and offer him there for a burnt offering upon one of the mountains which I will tell thee of" (Gen. 22:1-2). Never before in human history had God made such demand upon a person.

This unprecedented assignment must have thrown Abraham's mind into a paroxysm of confusion. Could it be that he had mistaken the instructions? Did God now approve of human sacrifice? What about the promise that Isaac, his only begotten son, would be the means of fulfilling the covenant that God had established with him?

Hebrews 11:17-19 indicates that Abraham reasoned through this issue by faith. He knew that God had never endorsed human sacrifice. He also knew that God, being righteous, was without iniquity, and being immutable, could not change or morph into something he was not. Furthermore, Abraham knew that God, being faithful, could not lie. God would keep his promise and Isaac would be the patriarch of the family (cf. Heb. 11:18). After working through these issues in his mind, Abraham concluded that this was a test,[1] or trial, of his faith. He determined to obey the Lord by faith, *"accounting that God was able to raise him up, even from the dead"* (Heb. 11:19a). So, he arose early the next morning, prepared for the journey, and set out for Moriah (cf. Gen. 22:3).

As father and son made the trek up the mountain, it was evident that they intended to offer a sacrifice as an act of worship. Abraham had told the servants at the base of the mountain that they were going to "worship" (Gen. 22:5). They carried with them fire and wood, two of the three items needed to make an offering. But one item was missing. Isaac raised the obvious question: *"Behold the fire and the wood: but where is the lamb for a burnt offering?"* (Gen. 22:7). Abraham's legendary

---

[1] The word "tempt" in verse one means "test."

reply contains profound theological significance: *"My son, God will provide* [jireh] *himself a lamb for a burnt offering"* (v. 8).

Jireh is a Hebrew verb meaning "to see" or "to provide." The connection between these two concepts may be discovered when a person considers the etymology of the word "provide." The prefix *pro-*, or *pre-*, means *before*. The Latin root *video* means *to see*. So, *providence* is essentially a matter of "seeing beforehand," or "foresight." God's *provision*, in other words, is based on his *prevision*, or capacity to see in advance, a need. When connected to the Divine name *Jehovah*, this verb means "The Lord will see to it," or "God's provision will be seen."

The dramatic account continues by noting Isaac's quiet submission to his father after Abraham reminds him that God would provide a lamb. Even when they came to the place, Isaac humbly resigns himself to being bound and laid upon the altar of wood. Then, the narrative peaks with this moment of tension and subsequent resolution:

And Abraham stretched for his hand, and took the knife to slay his son. And the angel of the Lord called unto him out of heaven, and said, Abraham, Abraham: and he said, Here am I. And he said, Lay not thine hand upon the lad, neither do thou any thing unto him: for now I know that thou fearest God, seeing thou hast not withheld thy son, thine only son from me. And Abraham lifted up his eyes, and looked, and behold behind him a ram caught in a thicket by his horns: and Abraham went and took the ram, and offered him up for a burnt offering in the stead of his son. And Abraham called the name of that place *Jehovah-jireh*: as it is said to this day, In the mount of the *LORD* it shall be seen. (Gen. 22:10-14)

The Geographical Setting

What is this reference to *"the mount of Jehovah"*? There is something especially intriguing about the geography in which this episode occurred. *Moriah*[2], itself, means "appearance of

Jehovah." The proper name indicates that it was a place in which a person might see a manifestation of the covenant, redeemer God. In fact, we might say concerning Moriah, "*In the mount of the LORD **HE** shall be seen*" [emphasis mine].

Moriah was a general area around Jerusalem characterized by various mountains and hills (cf. Gen. 22:2b; Ps. 125:2). Solomon's temple was built in Moriah at the very site that David had interceded to God and made a burnt offering on behalf of the people of Israel (cf. 1 Chr. 21:15 – 22:1; 2 Chr. 3:1). This magnificent temple became the site of the nation's sacrificial worship to Jehovah.

All of this is especially intriguing in light of the fact that Mount Calvary, the site of the crucifixion of Jesus Christ, was also in the Moriah Mountains. It is more than coincidental that certain Jewish rabbis explained Genesis 22:14—"*In the mount of Jehovah it shall be seen*"—in these terms: "God will see and choose that very place to cause his Shekinah[3] to rest thereon and to offer the offerings." Author Nathan Stone writes,

> Mount Moriah…became the site of Calvary and the scene of that grand and awful sacrifice of God's only begotten and well-beloved Son.[4]

The convergence at Moriah of each of these strategically important events, i.e. Abraham's sacrifice of his son Isaac, David's offering to stay God's judgment upon the covenant people, Solomon's temple and its sacrificial significance, and the substitutionary sacrifice of the Lord Jesus Christ on the cross, is, again, not a mere coincidence. Undoubtedly, the significance of this place in the Old Testament serves as a powerful type, or

---

[2] Note the *iah* suffix, coinciding with the *vah* (or *yah* in Yiddish) in the ineffable Name. Other examples of this suffix appear in names like *Isaiah, Jeremiah, Hezekiah, Elijah*, etc.

[3] A reference to the glory of God on display.

[4] Nathan Stone, *Names of God*, p. 67.

foreshadowing, of what would happen at the cross. But I get ahead of myself…

The Theological Significance

The account of Abraham and Isaac atop Mount Moriah and the name ascribed to God there is not simply an interesting and dramatic story from history. The name *Jehovah-Jireh*, God will provide, is theologically significant.

First, there is *a proverbial significance* to this name. Genesis 22:14 adds this interesting expression, "…*as it is said to this day*…" to indicate that there is an immediate application to be made from the revelation of this name. What happened at Moriah was, in other words, a proverb at that time and in subsequent generations.

When people in successive ages made reference to this episode, they did so in order to emphasize the truth that *Jehovah* is a God of providence. This incident stands as a perpetual reminder of the fact that God always provides for his covenant people. *Jehovah-Jireh*, in other words, reminds people in every age of time of the truth theologians call the *ordinary providence of God.*[5] The name is a proverb and a memorial to Divine providence.

It is, in fact, a valid proverb, or axiomatic truth, that the God who provided for Abraham in his moment of crisis will continue to provide for his people in every successive age. This account is designed to teach us that he is *Jehovah-Jireh* to us still, and we may trust him to be that in our various moments of crises as well. The late John Newton captures this thought in a beloved, old hymn:

---

[5] The adjective "ordinary" is used to distinguish it from the "extraordinary" providence. The first category speaks of God's involvement in the daily lives of his people, providing for them the necessities of life, or what Jacob once termed "the least of his mercies." The second category is employed to describe God's provision for the final blessedness and eternal security of his elect in Jesus Christ.

Though troubles assail and dangers affright;
Though friends should all fail, and foes all unite,
Yet one thing secures us, whatever betide:
The Scripture assures us, "The Lord will provide."

The birds, without barn or storehouse, are fed;
From them let us learn to trust for our bread;
His saints what is fitting shall ne'er be denied,
So long as 'tis written, "The Lord will provide."

His call we'd obey, like Abram of old;
Not knowing our way, but faith makes us bold;
For though we are strangers, we have a good Guide;
And trust in all dangers: "The Lord will provide."

When Satan appears to stop up our path,
And fills us with fears, we triumph by faith;
He cannot take from us, though oft' he has tried,
This heart-cheering promise, "The Lord will provide."

He tells us we're weak, our hope is in vain;
The good that we seek, we ne'er shall obtain;
But when such suggestions our faith thus have tried,
This answers all questions, "The Lord will provide."

No strength of our own nor goodness we claim;
Our trust is all thrown on Jesus' dear name.
In this our strong tower for safety we hide:
The Lord is our power, "The Lord will provide."

When life sinks apace and death is in view,
The word of his grace shall comfort us through;
Not fearing or doubting, with Christ on our side,
We hope to die shouting, "The Lord will provide."

Perhaps you are perplexed, however, at the very nature of this strange assignment. If God does not endorse human sacrifice, why would he call upon Abraham to offer the promised son to him on the altar? Well, God didn't want Isaac's life; he wanted Abraham's heart. This was a test to determine whether or not Abraham fully trusted the Lord to fulfill his promise. And it was a test to decipher which Abraham loved the most—the gift God had given him, or the God that gave the gift of a promised son.

Bible commentator Franz Delitzsch observes: *"One lesson this experience was intended to convey was that he should no more love his beloved son as his flesh and blood, but solely and only as the gracious gift and possession of God, as a good entrusted to him by God; which he was to be ready to render back to Him at any and every moment."*[6] In the Divine curricula for each of his servants, this lesson is one of the most important: Do we truly revere God and his claims upon our lives more than we value the people and things he has given us to enjoy? The Lord's word to us is, *"My son, give me thine heart"* (Pro. 23:26), and he intends to teach us the importance of total devotion to him, whatever the cost. Few, if any, will ever be tested as dramatically as Abraham was tried. But if he passed such a severe test of his faith, we may likewise succeed in putting God first and trusting him to be *Jehovah-Jireh* to us when we face lesser challenges.

There is one further lesson in terms of God's ordinary providence to highlight here. On a practical note, this account teaches us that when we look back, after the fact, on the trials of life, we may see something of God's greater purpose in the trial. Hindsight is 20/20, and reflection on a trial that I once thought would destroy me, reinforces my faith in him as I face the future. If this God of providence and grace was sufficient

---

[6] As quoted by Nathan Stone in *Names of God*, p. 82.

to help me through the crisis, then he is still enough to carry me through to the end.

Finally, there is not only a proverbial, but also *a prophetic significance* to this occasion. We see that fact in the futuristic language of verse fourteen: "*...it shall be seen*" (v. 14b). The clause indicates that there is a future application to be made from this name. The account of Abraham and Isaac on Mount Moriah, in other words, is not only commemorative of the past, but predictive of the future. The name *Jehovah-Jireh* is a prophecy of the truth theologians call the *extraordinary providence of God*.

As we previously noted, the proper noun *Moriah* means "Jehovah appears." The sentence "*In the mount of Jehovah it shall be seen*," therefore, may be rendered, "*In the mount of Jehovah **he** shall be seen*" [emphasis added]. A noted Jewish commentator translates this expression, "God will manifest himself to his people."

Could it be that Genesis 22:8 alludes to this thought, namely, that Moriah would prove to be the scene of a personal revelation of *Jehovah* to his people? When Abraham said, "*My son, God will provide himself a lamb for a burnt offering*," might it be that he is not only saying that God would provide the lamb, but that he would be the lamb provided? Without a doubt, the ram, i.e. male lamb, offered in the stead of Isaac prefigures the substitutionary sacrifice of the Lord Jesus Christ in the stead of his chosen people.

Abraham understood that this episode had a far deeper significance than a mere personal trial. To the challenge posed to Jesus by the unbelieving Jewish leaders, he replied, "*Your father Abraham rejoiced to see my day: and he saw it, and was glad*" (Jno. 8:56). Someone asks, "When did Abraham see the day of the Lord Jesus Christ?" We answer, "He saw it high atop Mt. Moriah when Isaac was set free and the lamb was offered in his place."

In that lamb, Abraham saw the Lamb of God who came to take away the sins of the world of God's elect (cf. Jno. 1:29), the Paschal Lamb sacrificed for us (cf. 1 Cor. 5:7b) and through whom we have been spared from the judgment of death. Here, he saw redemption by means of the precious blood of Christ, who was offered as *"lamb without blemish and without spot"* (cf. 1 Pet. 1:19). On an altar in Moriah, Abraham looked across the centuries to the great anti-type, the fulfillment of every sacrificial offering from Abel's lamb to the millions upon millions of lambs offered under the Jewish ceremonial system. Each of these sacrificial lambs typified the one sacrifice for sins forever that would be made by Jesus Christ, the Lamb of God. He saw the day of the Lord Jesus Christ, as he hung there on Calvary's hill, and it made him very glad. In fact, he rejoiced to see Christ's day.

The extraordinary provision of God for the redemption of his covenant people was nothing less than the substitutionary work of the Lord Jesus Christ. God did not withhold his only begotten and well-beloved Son. Motivated by nothing short of his own sovereign love (cf. Jno. 3:16), the Father freely delivered him up (cf. Acts 2:23), sparing not his own Son (cf. Rom. 8:32) for us. Further, Jesus voluntarily submitted himself to the work without a single word spoken in his own defense (cf. Is. 53:7; Acts 8:32; Phi. 2:7-8).

The doctrine of substitution is the very heart of the gospel. Paul puts it as follows: *"But God hath made him* [Christ] *to be sin for us, who knew no sin, that we might be made the righteousness of God in him"* (2 Cor. 5:21). What does the text mean? It means that the Lord Jesus was treated as if he had lived your life so you might be treated as if you had lived his life. He took the place of his people. Their sins were imputed, i.e. charged, against him, and his righteousness was credited to their account. Now when God looks at his elect by virtue of the substitutionary death of Jesus in their place, he sees them as righteous and fit for heaven.

The Swiss theologian Karl Barth (1886-1968), sometimes called "the greatest Protestant theologian of the 20th Century," once remarked that the greatest word in the New Testament was the little preposition *huper*, translated "for" in English, meaning "on behalf of." Jesus was made to be sin "on behalf of" his people. What was happening at the cross? The transaction at Calvary was an act of legal exchange and vicarious death, in which an innocent Lamb was provided in the stead of Isaac, if you will, so that Isaac (that is, the covenant sons and daughters of *Jehovah*) might be set free. Don't miss the biblically valid typology in this narrative. At the cross, God did, in fact, "see to it" that a provision was made for sinners.

The extraordinary providence of God in providing a remedy for sin guarantees his pledge to provide for the ordinary needs his children face in daily life: "*He that spared not his own Son, but delivered him up for us all, how shall he not with him freely give us all things?*" (Rom. 8:32). Do you want proof of God's promise to provide for you, my friend? Do you seek evidence that he is still *Jehovah-Jireh* today? Then, take another look at the cross. See Jehovah, your Savior, on Calvary's hill, the fulfillment of everything Moriah represented. The God who loved me enough to provide his very best for my eternal salvation surely loves me enough to provide for the daily necessities I face as I journey through this world on the way home.

Have you seen the cross? Have you learned that your God is *Jehovah-Jireh*? Then rejoice and be glad in the God who provides for your every need, both in time and eternity.

11
Jehovah-Rophe: The Lord our Healer

"...I am the LORD that healeth thee." (Exodus 15:26)

The compound names of *Jehovah* display the principle of progressive revelation in the Old Testament. In the unfolding revelation of the character of God to the Hebrew people, the Holy Spirit builds a case with each successive Divine name that *Jehovah* is capable of meeting every need that arises in the experience of his redeemed people. *Jehovah-Rophe*, the name we consider in this chapter, addresses our need for healing.

Rophe appears approximately 60 times in the Old Testament. The verb form means "to restore; to heal; to cure." The noun refers to the idea of a "physician." This soul-cheering name derives from the narrative of Exodus 15. Here we learn that *Jehovah* is the Healer of his people.

Historical Setting

Exodus 15 begins with the song of Moses celebrating deliverance from the Egyptians and the crossing of the Red Sea. Immediately upon the heels of deliverance, however, the nomads faced a grave challenge: *"...And they went three days in the wilderness, and found no water. And when they came to Marah, they could not drink of the waters of Marah, for they were bitter: therefore the name of it was called Marah. And the people murmured against Moses, saying, What shall we drink?"* (Ex. 15:22b-24).

Of course, drinking water is a necessity, but finding enough to sustain at least two million people, especially in the desert, would not be easy. The miraculous deliverance across the Red Sea and the conquest of the Egyptian army in the depths occurred only three days ago, but the present reality of parched throats and dehydration is proving to be a more powerful dynamic, eclipsing the joy of God's salvation and making it seem like a distant memory. When they finally found an oasis named *Marah*, the joy of discovery quickly turned to anger at the fact that the water was not potable.

Marah means "bitter." The locals had likely given the pond this name because it had long been unfit for human consumption. Perhaps it was contaminated with sulphur or some regional chemical. Maybe some animal had died in the pond and the multiplication of bacteria, without any regular rainfall, overwhelmed the ordinary, healing properties of nature. Whatever the reason the oasis was poisoned, it had long maintained this reputation.

Disappointment just compounded the misery of their thirst, and erupted in an expression of anger. The nation murmured and complained against Moses. Of course, in murmuring against Moses, they were effectively murmuring against the God who had so radically altered their circumstances. How quickly we forget the great things he has done! How slow we are to "connect the dots"! The God who raised up his servant Moses, decimated the Egyptian Empire with ten plagues, opened a safe passage for Israel in the sea, and defeated Pharoah and his six hundred chosen chariots beneath the flood, would surely make provision for a little detail like drinking water. That failure to think, and subsequently, to trust, explains the reason a murmuring and complaining spirit provokes the Lord to righteous anger (cf. 1 Cor. 10:10; Heb. 3:7-12).

When the people complained to Moses, he in turn took the need to the Lord: "*And he cried unto the LORD; and the LORD showed him a tree, which when he had cast into the waters, the waters were made sweet...*" (Ex. 15:25). Then, Moses employed the experience to teach a lesson, saying, "*If thou wilt diligently hearken to the voice of the LORD thy God, and wilt do that which is right in his sight, and wilt give ear to his commandments, and keep all his statutes, I will put none of these diseases upon thee, which I have brought upon the Egyptians: for I am the LORD that healeth thee* [Jehovah-Rophe]" (Ex. 15:26).

Just as God healed the polluted waters, so he pledges to provide healing to his people on the condition of their obedience to him. They would be spared the kind of diseases (or plagues) inflicted on the Egyptians. Israel's God is *Jehovah-Rophe*, the Lord who heals.

The Need for Healing

Why do human beings need a Healer? The need arises because disease and sickness, whether physical or spiritual (cf. 2 Jno. 3), is rife in this fallen world. According to the Bible, the pathogen of all disease is original sin (cf. Gen. 2:16-17; 3:16-19; Ecc. 12:3-7).

People need healing from both physical, or bodily, sickness and spiritual, or soul, sickness. In the Bible, physical disease takes many forms. There are skin diseases (e. g. wounds, bruises, sores [or ulcers], boils), internal diseases (e. g. leprosy, plagues, fever, infectious hemorrhages, cancer [or gangrene]), eye diseases (e. g. blindness, near-sightedness), heart disease and stroke, neurological and mental disorders (e. g. epilepsy, lunacy), orthopedic diseases (e. g. lameness, paralysis, muscle atrophy), digestive disorders, and more.

In Philippians 2:25-27, Paul mentions a member of the church at Philippi named Epaphroditus who was near death from fatigue/exhaustion (and probably dehydration). Timothy evidently suffered from a peptic stomach and a weakened immune system (cf. 1 Tim. 5:23). Trophimus had been left behind at Miletum due to an illness that prevented him from traveling (cf. 2 Tim. 4:20). Peter's mother-in-law was bedridden with a fever (cf. Mt. 8:14); Hezekiah was sick with a "pining sickness" (cf. Is. 38:9ff); Asa was diseased in both feet (cf. 2 Chr. 16:12-13); Job was covered in boils from the crown of his head to the sole of his feet (cf. Job 30:18); Paul had some kind of recurring physical pain that he describes as a painful "thorn in his flesh [body]" (cf. 2 Cor. 12:7); and there are many other similar examples.

Physical healing from sickness and disease is certainly possible, either directly (via immediate Divine intervention— cf. Lk. 8:43-48) or indirectly (via the medium of God's gift of medicine—cf. Lk. 10:34), but whether healing comes immediately or mediately, the ultimate source of this blessing is *Jehovah-Rophe*, the Lord our Healer.

James 5:14-18 indicates that there is a place for including prayer with physical therapy—i.e. the spiritual with the physiological—in dealing with bodily illness. Whether or not God is pleased to restore physical health to the infirm person, we may rely on the promise that "the prayer of faith will save the sick." Indeed, the deliverance pledged may not necessarily take the form of physical healing, but there will be a saving benefit in some helpful sense.

The bottom line is that perfect, physical health is not a promise for this life, but one reserved as a future prospect for the world to come; nevertheless, *Jehovah-Rophe* has promised to personally care for his children in their various trials with physical illness. Psalm 41:3 is such a promise: "*The LORD* [Jehovah] *will strengthen him upon the bed of languishing: thou wilt make all his bed in his sickness.*"

Perhaps the greatest threat to humanity is not the physical sickness that assaults the body but the spiritual disease that destroys the soul. Sin is compared to a disease in the Bible. Isaiah 1:5, for instance, describes the diseased condition of an apostate nation in these terms: "*The whole head is sick, and the whole heart faint. From the sole of the foot even unto the head, there is no soundness in it; but wounds, and bruises, and putrifying sores: they have not been closed, neither bound up, neither mollified with ointment.*"

Rebellion, idolatry, pride, malice, envy, lust, self-centeredness and other deformities of the soul because of sin are worse than diabetes, cancer, or emphysema. What a thrilling truth it is, however, that the Lord Jesus is the Healer of our spiritual maladies! The physical miracles Jesus performed during his public ministry were not only acts of mercy, but signs of his Messianic identity and manifestations of his power to heal the sickness of our souls. In this sense, he is still the Great Physician:

Is there no balm in Gilead; is there no physician there? Why then is not the health of the daughter of my people recovered? (Jer. 8:22)

The tree God showed to Moses that, when cast in, healed the bitter waters of Marah of their intrinsic poison, clearly prefigures the cross of Christ. It is the cross that sweetens the bitterness of our spiritual diseases. It is the cross alone that provides the antidote to the poison of sin. Isaiah 53:5 states clearly that Jesus Christ carried our pride, disobedience, jealousy and other spiritual "sicknesses" to the cross: "*But he was wounded for our transgressions, he was bruised for our iniquities: the chastisement of our peace was upon him; and with his stripes we are healed.*"

And the Lord Jesus still heals the maladies of his people that apply to him for a remedy: "*For I will restore health unto thee, and I will heal thee of thy wounds, saith the LORD; because they called thee an Outcast saying, This is Zion, whom no man seeketh after*" (Jer. 30:17); "*Moreover the light of the moon shall be as the light of the sun, and the light of the sun shall be sevenfold, as the light of seven days, in the day that the LORD bindeth up the breach of his people, and healeth the stroke of their wound*" (Is. 30:26).

He heals by granting forgiveness of their sins (cf. Ps. 103:3), and returning them from backsliding (cf. Jer. 3:22). He heals broken hearts (cf. Lk. 4:18), frequently by means of applying the healing balm of the gospel (cf. Lk. 5:31). *Jehovah-Rophe* still unstops deaf ears, opens blind eyes, strengthens lame feet, and cleansing leprous hearts (cf. Mt. 11:4-5). He is still the Sun of righteousness who arises upon his people with the healing rays of heavenly light (cf. Mal. 4:2).

Every other "physician"—whether modern science, humanistic philosophy, or secular culture—is a "physician of no value" (cf. Job. 13:4), offering only a partial alleviation of symptoms but not a radical cure of the cause of the problem (cf. Jer. 8:11). Only the Lord Jesus Christ deserves to be identified as the "tree of life whose leaves are for the healing of the nations" (Rev. 22:17). He alone is *Jehovah-Rophe*, the Lord our Healer.

12
Jehovah-Tsidkenu:
The Lord our Righteousness

"...and this is his name whereby he shall be called, THE LORD OUR RIGHTEOUSNESS." (Jeremiah 23:6b)

"...and this is the name wherewith she shall be called, The LORD our righteousness." (Jeremiah 33:16b)

Most of the prophetic books in the Old Testament contain a dual theme. First, and most prominent, is the *judgment motif*. As God's appointed prosecutors of the covenant, the prophets announced a coming judgment upon the disobedient nation, whether the northern kingdom of Israel or the southern kingdom of Judah, and upon other nations that had provoked him to anger. Before the prophecy is finished, however, each prophecy also contains a *restoration motif*, or message of hope for the future. Sometimes the promise of restoration is contingent on the nation's repentance (cf. Is. 55:7; Hos. 14:1-4), and sometimes Jehovah pledges to restore and revive them simply because it is his own sovereign pleasure to do so (cf. Eze. 34:19-31; 36:16-30). It is a great mercy that God through his prophets strikes a note of hope at the very moment he threatens to send the nation away into judgment.

Jeremiah's prophecy is no exception to this pattern of dual emphasis in prophetic literature. Far and away, the bulk of his prophecy announces the certainty of imminent judgment. Jeremiah announced the Divine sentence that Judah would be taken into Babylonian captivity (cf. 2 Kings 23:26-27). But he also predicted the restoration of God's covenant people under a righteous King he would elevate to the throne of David. His kingdom would be spiritual, not political, in nature, and it would be characterized by righteousness. Through this righteous

"Branch" (cf. Jer. 23:5) that God would cause to spring forth, His people would also be made righteous.

Chapters twenty-nine through thirty-three of Jeremiah's prophecy strike this more positive tone. These chapters are full of precious promises. Perhaps Jeremiah 31:17 conveys the hope for restoration from exile most succinctly: *"There is hope in thine end, saith the LORD, that thy children shall come again to their own border."*

The two verses that head this chapter—Jeremiah 23:6 and Jeremiah 33:16—record Holy Scripture's lone reference to the Divine name *Jehovah-Tsidkenu[1]*, which means "the Lord our Righteousness." Both passages appear in a *restoration* context, indicating that the revelation of this Divine name is connected to God's grace in the forgiveness of the sins of his people.

The Hebrew verb *tsedek* (or *zedek*), translated by the word "righteous," means "to be straight." It signifies something that is equal, or just. Interestingly, *tsedek* is the root of *Zedekiah*, the reigning king over Judah when Jeremiah penned his prophecy. *Zedekiah* means "Jehovah is righteous." When coupled with the name of God, *tsidkenu*, the expanded form of *tsedek*, takes the thought one step further. The Lord who is essentially righteous, in and of himself, also counts his people righteous in him. *Jehovah* is *our* righteousness. This is the ultimate expression of Divine grace.

Theological Significance

This sublime Divine name—*Jehovah-Tsidkenu*—is profoundly significant. In fact, it is central to the Christian gospel. What theological truth does it convey? It teaches the core *doctrine of justification*.

Justification might be defined as "the gracious act of a righteous God whereby he declares sinners just by means of the imputed righteousness of the Lord Jesus Christ." Romans 3:23-25

---

[1] Pronounced *zid'-kay-noo*

summarizes this doctrine succinctly: *"For all have sinned, and come short of the glory of God; being justified freely by his grace through the redemption that is in Christ Jesus: whom God hath set forth to be a propitiation through faith in his blood, to declare his righteousness for the remission of sins that are past, through the forbearance of God."*

Like many major Bible doctrines, *justification* is a word-picture. The image this forensic term suggests is the picture of a court proceeding, complete with a Judge at the bar, an alleged criminal in the dock, accused of violating a righteous law, a prosecutor equipped with condemning evidence, and an Advocate ready to stand in defense of the accused. In particular, *justification* has to do with the pronouncement of the final verdict. It is a "not guilty" verdict—a declaration of innocence and absolution of the indictment. But it is even more than that. *Justification* is a declaration of righteousness—a pronouncement that the individual once accused is everything that the law requires him to be. It is a legally-binding acknowledgement that he is "straight," or *zedek*, in line with every provision of the law.

The need for justification, then, might be explained in terms of this syllogism:

1. God is righteous and cannot countenance unrighteousness.
2. Man, because of sin, is not, in and of himself, righteous.
3. Therefore, God cannot countenance, or look with favor, upon man.

If man would be righteous, therefore, an alien righteousness, i.e. from an external source, must be imputed to his account before God will receive him favorably. It is this glorious gift of an imputed righteousness that is the thought expressed in the name, *Jehovah-Tsidkenu*.

Let's work through this sequence of thought. *First, the doctrine of justification begins with the affirmation that Jehovah is righteous, and cannot look with favor upon sin*. He

is the true "Zedekiah."[2] Righteousness, or justice, is the essence
of God's being, so that it is impossible for him to sin or err.
Consider these Biblical affirmations of the righteousness of God:

> He is the Rock, his work is perfect: for all his ways are
> judgment: a God of truth and without iniquity, just and right is
> he. (Deut. 32:4)

> Righteous art thou, O LORD, and upright are thy judgments. (Ps.
> 119:137)

> The Lord is righteous in all his ways, and holy in all his works.
> (Ps. 145:17)

How does the righteousness of God differ from the holiness of
God? Righteousness is a forensic, or legal, concept; holiness, an
ethical, or moral. God is both just and good in everything he
does. He never violates the principles of justice, for "*Justice and
judgment are the habitation of his throne*" (Ps. 89:14), nor the
standards of morality.

That is not always true among men. In our world, laws are
sometimes passed declaring a certain behavior "legal," howbeit
decent people know that even though it is legal, it remains
immoral. The unconscionable practice of abortion on demand in
the Western world is a classic example of this dichotomy
between what is legal and what is moral. With God, however,
there is never such polarity between morality and justice. His
holiness is equal to his righteousness, and his righteousness to his
holiness. There is no legal incongruity or moral deformity within
his Divine character.

***Secondly, the doctrine of justification proceeds to affirm
that, because of sin, man is not righteous by nature, and can
have no fellowship with a righteous God.*** Romans 3:10 defines

---

[2] Tha name means, again, "Jehovah is righteous."

the consequences of human depravity, stating unequivocally, *"There is none righteous; no, not one."* Paul reiterates the assertion, lest anyone accuse him of speaking in hyperbole. Every single one of Adam's natural offspring is naturally on the wrong side of God's law. There is no exception. Whether popes or paupers, presidents or peasants, rich or poor, male or female, adult or child, master or slave, well-know or unknown, Jew or Gentile—all have come short of God's glorious standard of righteousness because of sin; hence, the whole world is under Divine condemnation, "guilty before God" (cf. Rom. 3:18).

What apparent righteous deeds in human history someone might cite as evidence against the doctrine of total depravity are merely expressions of self-interest, self-protection, or self-preservation, for apart from the grace of God *"All our righteousnesses are as filthy rags; and we all do fade as a leaf; and our iniquities, like the wind, have taken us away"* (Is. 64:6). Because the righteous God *"desires truth* [justice; equity] *in the inward parts"* (cf. Ps. 51:6), then the motive, or intent, that drives the action must be right, as well as the action itself.

The bottom line is simply that human beings are in trouble. By virtue of Adam's transgression, the entire human family has been plunged into a state of alienation from God. The righteous God can never enter into union with unrighteous men. It would violate his own righteous character to do so.[3]

Yet, in spite of the fact of human condemnation, there is evidence that God blesses people. Job said, *"I know it is so of a truth, but how can man be just with God?"* (Job 9:2). I cannot think of a more important question. How might sinful men be right with God?

Job indicates, however, that people are evidently counted as such. "I know that men are counted as just before God," he says, "but I cannot tell how it is so." How did he know that God

---

[3] See Habakkuk 1:14, 2 Corinthians 6:14b-16a, and Hebrews 1:9a as proof texts.

considered certain people to be righteous? In a word, Job saw God blessing people. He, himself, had been abundantly blessed by God, and others around him were also recipients of the smiles of Divine providence. Of course, the righteous God does not bless unrighteous sinners. So, he knew by empirical evidence of Divine blessing upon their lives that some men were counted as righteous, but he couldn't determine how that might be.

Bildad asked the same question in Job 25:4. After describing the majesty and power of God, he queries, "*How then can man be justified with God? Or how can he be clean that is born of a woman? Behold even to the moon, and it shineth not; yea, the stars are not pure in his sight. How much less man, that is a worm? And the son of man, which is a worm?*" This is the "sixty-four million dollar question." It is a question that echoes throughout the corridors of history.

Is there an answer to this highest of mysteries? Indeed, there is. The answer is concealed in this Divine name, *Jehovah-Tsidkenu,* and revealed in the gospel message of justification by an imputed righteousness. That brings us to the third, and final, feature of this sublime doctrine.

Thirdly, the doctrine of justification affirms that God has provided righteousness to his elect through the imputed righteousness of the Lord Jesus Christ, who fulfilled the precept of the law and satisfied the penalty of the law, in their stead. This emphasis is the heart and soul of the Christian gospel. It is the trumpet blast of the church of God. Consider these verses that teach that our righteousness is in the Lord alone and what he has done for us:

> Surely, shall one say, In the LORD have I righteousness and strength: even to him shall men come; and all that are incensed against him shall be ashamed. In the LORD shall all the seed of Israel be justified, and shall glory. (Is. 45:24-25)

...This is the heritage of the servants of the LORD, and their righteousness is of me, saith the LORD. (Is. 54:17b)

Therefore as by the offence of one judgment came upon all men to condemnation; even so by the righteousness of one the free gift came upon all men unto justification of life. For as by one man's disobedience many were made sinners, so by the obedience of one shall many be made righteous. (Rom. 5:18-19)

But of him are ye in Christ Jesus, who of God is made unto us wisdom, and righteousness, and sanctification, and redemption: that, according as it is written, He that glorieth, let him glory in the Lord. (1 Cor. 1:30-31)

For he hath made him to be sin for us, who knew no sin; that we might be made the righteousness of God in him. (2 Cor. 5:21)

What do these thrilling verses mean? They teach that Jesus Christ assumed the role as the legal substitute on behalf of those that were given to him in the covenant of redemption; he bore their sins in his own body on the cross, suffering the punishment due to those sins in himself, and paying the price for their redemption. In exchange, his perfect obedience to God's law throughout his righteous life was credited to their account so that now, when the Judge of all the earth looks upon them, he sees them as perfectly righteous, blameless and pure. He is our righteousness, our only righteousness, our complete righteousness.

Did you notice the subtle change in the two verses that head this chapter? The two verses, ten chapters and ten verses apart, are virtually identical. Jeremiah 33:16 is a verbatim quote of Jeremiah 23:6...with one exception. The sole discrepancy is in the pronoun. Jeremiah 23:6 reads, *"This is the name whereby **he** shall be called, The LORD OUR RIGHTEOUSNESS* [Jehovah-Tsidkenu]," but Jeremiah 33:16 read, *"This is the name* *wherewith **she** shall be called, the LORD our righteousness* [Jehovah-Tsidkenu]."

Is that a misprint? Did some scribe mistakenly include the letter "s"? Not at all. This is simply a case in which the bride assumes her husband's name in marriage. The bride of Christ is given his name by virtue of the everlasting covenant. His righteousness has now been imputed to her.

Now, no charge may be levied against the people of God, for their sins have been removed from them as far as the east is from the west (cf. Ps. 103:12). Hence, the old prophets could say, "*He hath not beheld iniquity in Jacob, neither hath he seen perverseness in Israel,*" (Num. 23:21a), and "*In those days, and in that time, saith the LORD, the iniquity of Israel shall be sought for, and there shall be none; and the sins of Judah, and they shall not be found: for I will pardon them whom I reserve*" (Jer. 50:20). And all those who believe these glad tidings may say with Isaiah, "*I will greatly rejoice in the LORD, my soul shall be joyful in my God; for he hath clothed me with the garments of salvation, he hath covered me with the robe of righteousness...*" (Is. 61:10), and with the apostle Paul, "*Who shall lay anything to the charge of God's elect? It is God that justifieth. Who is he that condemneth? It is Christ that died, yea rather, that is risen again, who is even at the right hand of God, who also maketh intercession for us*" (Rom. 8:33-34).

Because we know our God as *Jehovah-Tsidkenu*, the Lord our righteousness, we may also sing with the hymwriter this song of true gospel experience:

I once was a stranger to grace and to God,
I knew not my danger, and felt not my load;
Though friends spoke in rapture of Christ on the tree,
Jehovah-tsidkenu meant nothing to me.

When free grace awoke me, by light from on high,
Then legal fears shook me, I trembled to die;

> No refuge, no safety, in self could I see;
> *Jehovah-tsidkenu* my Savior must be.
>
> My terrors all vanished before the sweet name;
> My guilty fears banished, with boldness I came
> To drink at the fountain, life-giving and free;
> *Jehovah-tsidkenu* is all things to me.

As for me, my hope is founded on this solid Rock alone—the firm foundation of Jesus' blood and righteousness. All other ground is sinking sand.

13
Jehovah-Shalom: The Lord our Peace

"Then Gideon built an altar there unto the LORD, and called it Jehovah-shalom: unto this day it is yet in Ophrah of the Abiezrites." (Judges 6:24)

The biblical concept of *peace* is frequently connected to the concept of *righteousness*, the theme of the previous chapter. The sequence of the two terms, however, is significant. It is never peace that leads to righteousness; instead, righteousness promotes and effects peace. Consider these verses that serve to illustrate the sequence in which the terms appear together:

Mercy and truth are met together; righteousness and peace have kissed each other. (Ps. 85:10)

And the work of righteousness shall be peace; and the effect of righteousness quietness and assurance for ever. And my people shall dwell in a peaceable habitation, and in sure dwellings, and in quiet resting places. (Is. 32:17-18)

For the kingdom of God is not meat and drink; but righteousness, and peace, and joy in the Holy Ghost. (Rom. 14:17)

To whom also Abraham gave a tenth part of all; first being by interpretation King of righteousness, and after that also King of Salem, which is, King of peace. (Heb. 7:2)

The sequential connection of these twin concepts—i.e. righteousness and peace—then, leads us now to consider another Divine name, *Jehovah-Shalom*, the Lord our Peace, on the heels of the study on *Jehovah-Tsidkenu*, the Lord our Righteousness. It is a fact that knowing God as our righteousness is prerequisite to knowing him as our peace.

Historical Background

The time of the Judges in the history of the nation of Israel was a very turbulent period. These were days of anarchy, when *"every man did that which was right in his own eyes"* (Jud. 21:25). Though the nation inhabited the promised land, social and moral chaos prevailed. The book describes a series of cycles. God blessed the people with prosperity; the affluent people forgot the Lord and provoked him to anger; they were sold into bondage to some neighboring regime; they cried to the Lord for help in their extremity; he raised up a "judge" to deliver them from the hand of the enemy; God again blessed the people with prosperity, and the cycle began all over again.

It is in the alternating prosperity/adversity, slavery/deliverance motifs and the tone of general restlessness described in *Judges* that God is revealed as *Jehovah-Shalom*, the Lord our Peace. The first and only occurrence of this name is in the narrative of Judges 6. For seven years, the Midianites oppressed Israel. The nation had no peace. But God called an unlikely character named Gideon to deliver his people from the Midianites. Once convinced that *Jehovah* had in fact appeared to him for the sake of his people, Gideon built an altar to express his faith that the Lord would restore peace. He called it *Jehovah-Shalom* (Jud. 6:24).

Theological Significance

Although this name only appears once in Scripture, it expresses a theological truth that is pervasive in both Testaments. *Jehovah-Shalom* is significant because it teaches the *doctrine of reconciliation*, one of the key words of the Christian gospel.

The familiar Hebrew word *shalom* is rich with significance. It means "peace, or harmony" and derives from a concept that signifies "rest from war." It speaks of physical or spiritual "wholeness" or "completeness" and expresses the thought of "contentment and satisfaction in life;" hence, *shalom* is used as the regular salutation when Jewish people both greet one another and depart company.

The Bible teaches that *Jehovah*, himself, is the source of all true peace. Consider the following verses:

The LORD will give strength unto his people; the LORD will bless his people with peace. (Ps. 29:11)

LORD, thou wilt ordain peace for us: for thou hast wrought all our works in us. (Is. 26:12)

The LORD lift up his countenance upon thee, and give thee peace. (Num. 6:26)

Jehovah, alone gives us rest from our enemies: "*But when ye go over Jordan, and dwell in the land which the LORD your God giveth you to inherit, and when he giveth you rest from all your enemies round about, so that ye dwell in safety; then there shall be a place which the LORD your God shall choose to cause his name to dwell there...*" (Deut. 12:10-11a). For this reason, the New Testament twice speaks of him as the "God of Peace":

Now the God of peace be with you all. Amen. (Rom. 15:33)

Now the God of peace, that brought again from the dead our Lord Jesus, that great shepherd of the sheep, through the blood of the everlasting covenant... (Heb. 13:20)

True, lasting peace derives only from this God of Peace and the Lord Jesus Christ, the "Prince of Peace" (cf. Is. 9:6). "Peace on earth" will never be achieved by political or legislative solution. Jesus Christ is the sole source of peace in this world. He is our *Jehovah-Shalom*.

World peace, in fact, is an optical illusion. This planet has been a theater of conflict and disunity since the fall of man in the Garden of Eden, and will continue to be such until the Lord Jesus returns. God's people, however, may have peace and quietness in their hearts, even in the midst of the troubles and conflicts of life, when they believe the message know as "the gospel of peace" (Rom. 10:15; Eph. 6:15).

The apostle Paul said it like this: "*Therefore being justified by faith, we have peace with God through our Lord Jesus Christ*" (Rom. 5:1). In believing, God's children are filled with a peace that passes understanding, i.e. a peace the world can never possibly know: "*Now the God of hope fill you with all joy and peace in believing, that ye may abound in hope, through the power of the Holy Ghost*" (Rom. 15:13; cf. Heb. 4:11; Phi. 4:7).

This inward peace might be described as a "rest from war in the midst of war." Though dangers surround the child of grace, quiet peace may prevail in the depths of his soul. Like the ocean waters deep below the surface are calm and serene, though the waters above are tempest tossed, so *Jehovah-Shalom* gives "perfect peace" to the individual whose eye of faith is fixed upon him (cf. Is. 26:3). No doubt, this must have been the experience of Gideon of old, and the reason he named the newly-constructed altar "The Lord is our peace."

Of course, experiential peace in the heart is not possible to anyone except those who have previously been reconciled to God at the cross. Subjective peace, in other words, is impossible unless objective peace has been accomplished by the Lord Jesus Christ. The wicked, i.e. those who are not God's children, can never know peace: "*There is no peace, saith my God, to the wicked*" (Is. 57:21).

The biblical doctrine of reconciliation is the great truth that Jesus Christ satisfied the righteous wrath of God against sin on behalf of his people, so making everlasting peace. The verb "to reconcile" means to replace enmity with amity. It is a relational term, indicating a relationship that was once breached by offense and has now been repaired. The doctrine consists of two important parts: *propitiation*, or the removal of Divine wrath, and *expiation*, or the removal of man's sin which necessitated that wrath.

The gospel is "the word of reconciliation" (cf. 2 Cor. 5:19b). It reports the good news that Jesus Christ has already accomplished the work of reconciliation: *"And all things are of God, which hath reconciled us to himself by Jesus Christ...to wit, that God was in Christ, reconciling the world unto himself, not imputing their trespasses unto them..."* (2 Cor. 5:18a, 19a). Whether or not a person believes the word of reconciliation does not change the fact that the work of reconciliation is already finished. Whether or not, in other words, the born again child of God ever experiences subjective peace with God in his own conscience— an experience Scripture calls the "assurance of salvation"—God is already at peace with all his elect by virtue of the work of peace-making Jesus accomplished in their stead.

Paul, the theological champion of the New Testament, describes the finished work of reconciliation at the cross: *"And having made peace through the blood of his cross, by him to reconcile all things unto himself; by him, I say, whether they be things in earth, or things in heaven. And you, that were sometime alienated and enemies in your mind by wicked works, yet now hath he reconciled in the body of his flesh through death, to present you holy and unblameable and unreproveable in his sight"* (Col. 1:20-22). Notice the past tense: "He hath reconciled." Reconciliation is a settled fact, regardless of man's response to the report of that fact in the preaching of the gospel. If Jesus reconciled sinners to God, then they are reconciled and God is at peace with them. Although God was angry with them, his anger has been turned away by the ultimate peace-offering of all time, the precious blood of the Lord Jesus Christ (cf. Is. 12:1).

Note also in this passage the reason reconciliation is necessary. Sin is the cause of man's alienation from God. Because of sin, mankind is naturally God's enemy. The offending party in this relational alienation is man; the offended party is God. By nature, human beings are "enemies in their minds by wicked works" (Col. 1:21), that is, enemies in opposition to God: *"Because the carnal mind is enmity[1] against God: for it is not subject to the law of God, neither indeed can be"* (Rom. 8:7). The good news, however, is that Jesus Christ has made peace on behalf of his chosen people: *"For if, when we were enemies, we were reconciled to God by the death of his Son, much more, being reconciled, we shall be saved by his life"* (Rom. 5:10).

The natural man is not merely indifferent to God. His problem is not simple passivity or disinterest in the things of God. He is actively hostile toward God. He hates God and would gladly unseat him from his heavenly throne if he could. That God would then initiate reconciliation with such wretched sinners is truly an act of his amazing grace.

Jesus Christ did not make peace by striking a compromise between the two antithetical parties. He did not simply negotiate a truce, asking God to lower his expectations a bit and asking man to increase his efforts at good behavior. No, the Lord our Peacemaker affected reconciliation by incarnating the offense. As the one Mediator between God and men, the man Christ Jesus assumed the punishment due to the sins of all who had been given to him in covenant by the Father, and by his one offering for sins forever, satisfied the demands of Divine justice. In so doing, he put the sins of his people away "as far as the east is from the west" (cf. Ps. 103:12). Our "Daysman"[2] laid his hand upon God, for he verily is God, and upon offending man, for he assumed our human nature, in order to repair the relationship between God and his people that had been broken by sin (cf. Job 9:33).

Now, Jesus Christ is *Jehovah-Shalom* to us, not only in terms of the vertical relationship between God and his children, but even in terms of the horizontal relationships between us and our

---

[1] *Enmity* refers to "hostility, antagonism, animosity."
[2] Arbiter, umpire, mediator

fellow man. Paul argued this point in Ephesians 2 to encourage Jewish and Gentile believers to put away their ethnic, tribal, cultural, linguistic, political, social and economic differences and to live in peace in the New Testament Church: *"For he is our peace, who hath made both* [that is, Jew and Gentile] *one, and hath broken down the middle wall of partition between us; having abolished in his flesh the enmity, even the law of commandments contained in ordinances, for to make in himself of twain one new man, so making peace; and that he might reconcile both unto God in one body by the cross, having slain the enmity thereby: and came and preached peace to you which were afar off* [i.e. Gentiles], *and to them that were nigh* [i.e. Jews]." (Eph. 2:14-17).

When a believer understands the finished work of reconciliation Jesus accomplished at the cross, in other words, he discovers peace in his own heart. Such peace, consequently, spills over into his relationships, even in the church (cf. Col. 3:15), so that we may have fellowship with God and with one another through our *Jehovah-Shalom*, the Lord who is our Peace.

The call of discipleship to imitate the Father (cf. Eph. 5:1; Mt. 5:48), then, is a call to be peacemakers: *"Blessed are the peacemakers: for they shall be called the children of God"* (Mt. 5:9). May the God who is your peace bless you to spread that peace into the relationships in your life, first in the home, then in the local church, and finally, as much as is possible, with all men.

14
Jehovah-M'Kaddesh:
The Lord Who Sanctifies

"And ye shall keep my statutes, and do them: I am the LORD which sanctify you." (Leviticus 20:8)

S*imul justus et peccator*, a Latin phrase likely popularized by Martin Luther, is translated "At the same time, just and sinful." I mention it because, like the last chapter and its connection to chapter 12, this expression connects the Divine name we now consider to *Jehovah-Tsidkenu*, the theme of chapter 12.

Jehovah-Tsidkenu, again, reveals the Lord as our righteousness. We are just (a synonym for "righteous") because the righteousness of the Lord Jesus Christ has been imputed to our account at the cross. But though we have been justified by grace alone and thereby given a legal status of righteousness before Heaven's bar, we are yet sinful in our daily lives, struggling with "the flesh"[1] in actual practice. In a word, we are simultaneously just and sinful—*simul justus et peccator*; hence, God's people need sanctification as well as justification.

Biblical Origin of the Name

We can be thankful, therefore, that God reveals himself in Scripture not only as *Jehovah-Tsidkenu*, the Lord our righteousness, but also as *Jehovah-M'Kaddesh*, the Lord who sanctifies. The name originates with the instructions God gave to the Levitical priests regarding the pattern of Divine worship: *"And ye shall keep my statutes, and do them: I am the LORD which sanctify you* [Jehovah-M'Kaddesh]" (Lev. 20:8).

---

[1] The word *sarx*, translated "flesh" in the Pauline epistles, frequently refers to the old, fallen nature, or the principle of indwelling sin.

The book of *Leviticus* is the worship manual of ancient Israel. It is filled with detailed instructions about how to conduct worship, which sacrifices were appropriate for each occasion, how the sacrifice was to be prepared and offered, who was qualified to make the various offerings, which garments were to be worn during the offering, what conditions were necessary in order for worshippers to approach God, how to consecrate someone anew for worship who had become ceremonially unclean, and numerous other specific regulations for life in and around the tabernacle. If a person doubts that God is serious about how worship should be conducted, he merely needs to review the book of *Leviticus*.

Why, someone questions, is God so particular about the transportation of the tabernacle, the sequence in which it is to be erected, the layout of the furniture, the vestments of the priests, the occasion for the various offerings, the arrangement of the annual worship calendar, the parts of the animal that were to be washed, burnt in sacrifice or saved for consumption by the priests, and the many other specifics related to Levitical service? Does it really matter that every little detail be observed precisely as God prescribed? Wouldn't it be just the same if the priests simply observed most of the Divine regulations, even if they left off a detail here, or substituted an item there?

Ask Nadab and Abihu how serious it is to experiment with the Divine plan. These two sons of Aaron conspired together to innovate with God's pattern. Perhaps they were bored with the simplicity of the worship routines. Maybe they thought they could improve on the Lord's arrangement. Or possibly, they just didn't think it mattered that much to do everything exactly as God had said. Whatever their motive, they offered "strange fire" upon the altar, and were struck dead on the spot (cf. Lev. 10:1-2).

Do we think God's response to the maverick boys was a bit extreme—that the punishment didn't quite fit the crime? Aaron must have agreed, for Moses said unto him, "*This is it that the*

LORD spake, saying, I will be sanctified in them that come nigh me, and before all the people I will be glorified. And Aaron held his peace" (Lev. 10:3).

What does Jehovah mean by the clause, "I will be sanctified"? He means, "I will be regarded as holy; I will be reverenced; I intend to be taken seriously." If there was ever any doubt prior to this time that the Lord meant business—that he refused to be trifled with—this episode removed all doubt. The holiness of God was to be respected in every part of daily life and the way the people approached him in worship set the pace for that reality.

On the heels of the death of Aaron's two sons, the Lord reinforced this lesson on the priority of holiness to him: "*Do not drink wine nor strong drink, thou, nor thy sons with thee, when ye go into the tabernacle of the congregation, lest ye die...that ye may put difference between holy and unholy, and between unclean and clean; and that ye may teach the children of Israel all the statutes which the LORD hath spoken unto them by the hand of Moses*" (Lev. 10:8-11).

The Divine regulations imposed on the priesthood in Divine worship were intended to stress the importance of making distinctions between the holy and the profane. God intended his people to learn to make value judgments in every circumstance of daily life, affirming what God approves and denying what he prohibits.

The theme of *Leviticus*, then, with its elaborate detail for conducting Divine worship and exact requirements for every facet of daily life (including personal hygiene, dietary regulations, waste disposal, sexual ethics, criteria for diagnosing and treating infectious diseases, and more) is *sanctification*, or holiness. Strict adherence to the Divine pattern is the purpose for the frequent repetition of the sentence "*I am the LORD that sanctifieth you*" in this book. Seven times in Leviticus 20-22, in fact, God refers to himself as *Jehovah-M'Kaddesh*.

The Priority of Holiness

The verb "to sanctify" refers to the separation and consecration of something for special use. Both in the Old Testament and the New, the important English nouns "sanctification" and "holiness" derive from the same Hebrew and Greek roots.[2] The terms mean, literally, "to distinguish, or differentiate." When an item is "sanctified" or made "holy," it is set aside from everything mundane and routine so that it might be devoted to God and his service.

Let me illustrate the concept. When I was just a boy, my mother would sometimes bake a cake or pie on Saturday in preparation for a fellowship meal after morning worship on Sunday, a tradition many Baptists know as "dinner on the grounds." She would frequently instruct my two brothers and I when it was finished, "Boys, don't touch this cake. I made it for lunch after church tomorrow." We knew that it was off-limits, no matter how tempting it might be to three hungry boys, for she had "set it apart" for a particular use. That cake had been sanctified.

That which is holy (or sanctified), then, is *different* from everything else around it. It is not ordinary or commonplace; it is extraordinary because it has been distinguished and dedicated to a noble purpose. Furthermore, it is God that determines what is holy.

The sanctity of the Sabbath in creation is an example of God setting aside one day from the other six days of the week as a day of rest: "*And God blessed the seventh day, and sanctified it: because that in it he had rested from all his work which God created and made*" (Gen. 2:3). This rhythm of work and rest built into the very fabric of the natural order was intended for man's benefit: "*The sabbath was made for man, and not man for the sabbath*" (Mr. 2:27). As such, the Creator's act of separating one

---

[2] In Old Testament Hebrew, both terms stem from *qodesh*; in New Testament Greek, both derive from *hagios*.

day each week from the other six is an example of his goodness and concern for the man and woman that he made.

Not only does God sanctify time, he also sanctifies places. The Hebrew word *mikdash* (as in *Jehovah-M'Kaddesh*) is the root of the words variously translated *tabernacle*, *temple*, and *sanctuary* in the Old Testament. Of course, the tabernacle, the temple and the sanctuary were holy places, set apart for the worship of *Jehovah* under the Mosaic Covenant. Even today, Christians frequently refer to the place of worship within a church building as a "sanctuary"—sacred space set aside for the worship of God.

In addition to these concepts of sacred time and sacred space, people are sometimes described as sanctified, or distinguished from other people for a holy (or Divinely ordained) purpose. Consider as an example of a holy person the intriguing role of the Nazarite within Jewish culture.

The law of the Nazarite is given in Numbers 6. Notice the frequent use of the word "separation" in describing this individual:

> "When either man or woman shall separate themselves to vow a vow of a Nazarite, to separate themselves unto the LORD: He shall separate himself from wine and strong drink, and shall drink no vinegar of wine, or vinegar of strong drink, neither shall he drink any liquor of grapes, nor eat moist grapes, or dried...And the Nazarite shall shave the head of his separation at the door of the tabernacle of the congregation, and shall take the hair of the head of his separation, and put it in the fire which is under the sacrifice of the peace offerings..." (Num. 6:2-3, 18).

Speaking candidly, Nazarites stood out from ordinary culture like the proverbial sore thumb. It was impossible to overlook them. These woolly-boogers with their long beards, dreadlocked hair, ethic of abstinence from everything connected to the fruit of the vine (a staple of Jewish culture), and refusal to have any physical contact with a dead body were different enough to make them conspicuous. I'm sure every little child pointed a finger when he saw a Nazarite, asking his parent in a loud voice, "Abba! What is wrong with that man?"

Do you think the parent gently scolded the child and said, "Don't point, son"? As a matter of fact, probably not. You see, a Nazarite was not like some strangely-dressed person one might see at the local mall. A Nazarite's appearance was not a personal expression of his "individuality." He looked radically different from everyone else not because he was revolting against social norms or struggling with an identity crisis.

Instead, God called the Nazarite to be an object lesson to the rest of the nation for the priority of sanctification. His unusual appearance was Divinely-prescribed to remind Israel that they were called to be a holy people, different from the nations around them. An orthodox Hebrew parent, therefore, would not have tried to silence his inquisitive child. He would have said, "I'm so glad you asked, son; this man's strange appearance is a real-life illustration God has provided us to teach us that we are not supposed to be like others, but to follow and obey the Lord."

This passage from Leviticus 20 spells out God's call to separation unto his covenant people:

> Ye shall not walk in the manners of the nation, which I cast out before you: for they committed all these things, and therefore I abhorred them. But I have said unto you, Ye shall inherit their land, and I will give it unto you to possess it, a land that floweth with milk and honey: I am the LORD your God, which have separated you from other people. Ye shall therefore put difference between clean beasts and unclean, and between unclean fowls and clean: and ye shall not make your souls abominable by beast, or by fowl, or by any manner of living thing that creepeth on the ground, which I have separated from you as unclean. And ye shall be holy unto me: for I the LORD am holy, and have severed you from other people, that ye should be mine. (Lev. 20:23-26)

The call to non-conformity in the Christian gospel is, likewise, a call to be different from the world: "*And be not conformed to this world: but be ye transformed by the renewing of your mind, that ye may prove what is that good, and acceptable, and perfect, will of God*" (Rom. 12:2); "*Wherefore come out from among them, and be ye separate, saith the Lord, and touch not the unclean thing; and I will receive you, and will be a Father unto you, and ye shall be my sons and daughters, saith the Lord Almighty*" (2 Cor. 6:17-18). Sanctification, then, is the will of God for believers today, just as it was for his people in olden times (cf. 1 Ths. 4:3).

Likewise, God called upon the Israelites to "sanctify" to him every firstborn, whether among their livestock or their human offspring, saying "It is mine" (Ex. 13:2). Each was to be consecrated to him, indicating their understanding of and submission to Jehovah's priority in their lives.

Not only did God set aside certain groups, like the Nazarites or the firstborn, consecrating them to his service, he also sanctified individuals for a particular task. To the prophet Jeremiah, God said, "*Before I formed thee in the belly I knew thee; and before thou camest forth out of the womb I sanctified thee, and I ordained thee a prophet unto the nations*" (Jer. 1:5). Again, here is evidence that it is the Lord that determines what is holy and distinguishes it from the profane.

Theological Significance

Why is holiness so important to God? The answer is because Jehovah, himself, is holy. In fact, he alone is intrinsically holy in and of himself. He alone is the source and origin of holiness, in other words. Holiness always derives from the God who is essentially holy; it is never conferred upon him: "*There is none holy as the LORD; for there is none beside thee: neither is there any rock like our God*" (1 Sam. 2:2); "*Who shall not fear thee, O Lord, and glorify thy name? for thou only art holy: for all nations shall come and worship before thee; for thy judgments are made manifest*" (Rev. 15:4).

Unlike most of the other attributes of God, holiness is more an umbrella concept—a composite attribute that includes and encompasses all the rest. Everything true about God, in other words, is bathed in holiness; hence, the most frequent adjective attached to the name of the Lord, or his Divine character, is "holy": "*He sent redemption unto his people; he hath commanded his covenant for ever; holy and reverend is his name*" (Ps. 111:9; cf. Lev. 22:32; 1 Chr. 16:10; Ps. 33:21; Ps. 99:3; Ps. 103:1; Ps. 145:21; Is. 57:15). In fact, the seraphim around the heavenly throne sing in perpetual, antiphonal song, "*Holy, holy, holy, is the LORD of hosts: the whole earth is full of his glory*" (Is. 6:3).

What does it mean when Scripture says that God is holy? It means that he is different and distinct from everyone and everything else in the universe. He is separate from sin and transcendent to his creation. Because God alone is essentially holy, he is the source of everything else that is holy. Holiness is conferred by God. Everything that comes into contact with this holy God is, consequently, holy: "*Thus saith the LORD; I am returned unto Zion, and will dwell in the midst of Jerusalem: and Jerusalem shall be called a city of truth; and the mountain of the LORD of hosts the holy mountain*" (Zech. 8:3). Further, it means that this holy God requires holiness from his people who presume to draw nigh to him: "*Speak unto all the congregation of the children of Israel, and say unto them, Ye shall be holy: for I the LORD your God am holy*" (Lev. 19:2).

The problem is, however, that people are not naturally holy. In fact, human beings are defiled and polluted by sin. But there is good news. *Jehovah-M'Kaddesh*, the Lord who sanctifies, undertakes, as a gift of his sovereign grace, to sanctify the objects of his everlasting love.

Every provision of the everlasting covenant aims to make them holy. Election is to the ultimate intent that those chosen might stand before him *"holy and without blame, in love"* (Eph. 1:4). Further, all who are chosen by the Father are made ***positionally holy*** by means of the sacrificial offering of the Lord Jesus Christ on the cross: *"By the which will we are sanctified through the offering of the body of Jesus Christ once for all"* (Heb. 10:10); *"Wherefore Jesus also, that he might sanctify the people with his own blood, suffered without the gate"* (Heb. 13:12).

Just as the Lord Jesus is "our righteousness," he is also "our sanctification" (cf. 1 Cor. 1:30); therefore, when addressing the Church of God at Corinth, the apostle employs the aorist tense to indicate a past act of grace with ongoing results, writing *"to them that are sanctified in Christ Jesus"* (1 Cor. 1:2). The verb *are sanctified* indicates that they are presently in possession of holiness by virtue of their union with Jesus Christ in his death.

Then, those set apart as God's elect people in the covenant of grace, and sanctified by Jesus Christ in a positional sense at the cross, are further made ***vitally holy***, really and personally, in the work of regeneration. When Paul writes that God's people are saved and *"called with a holy calling, not according to"* their works, *"but according to his own purpose and grace which was given us in Christ Jesus before the world began"* (2 Tim. 1:9), he refers to the effectual call of the Holy Spirit, or the God's gift of regenerating grace in the heart. It is a "holy calling," because it derives from a holy God and has the effect of making the recipient holy. In fact, the new nature created in God's child at regeneration is *"created in righteousness and true holiness"* (cf. Eph. 4:24).

This new identity in Christ, or the new nature, cannot sin, for it is truly holy: *"Whosoever is born of God doth not commit sin; for his seed remaineth in him and he cannot sin, because he is born of God"* (1 Jno. 3:9). Granted, the old, sinful nature with which a person is born into this world is not eradicated by the new birth. It remains just as depraved and corrupt as it ever was, necessitating "a continual and irreconcilable warfare" between the flesh—i.e. the old nature—and the spirit—i.e. the new nature, as long as mortal life remains. There is something within the born again child of grace, however, that is really and personally holy.

Finally, *Jehovah-M'Kaddesh* has made provision to make his elected, redeemed and born again children **perfectly holy** when Jesus Christ our Lord returns: "*And the very God of peace sanctify you wholly; and I pray God your whole spirit and soul and body be preserved blameless unto the coming of our Lord Jesus Christ*" (1 Ths. 5:23). Indeed, the Lord, and the Lord alone, sanctifies his people.

In the meantime as we wait for final and entire sanctification at the Savior's second coming, the people God has "set apart" by grace unto himself are called to be **practically holy** in conduct and life: "*But as he which hath called you is holy, so be ye holy in all manner of conversation; because it is written, Be ye holy; for I am holy*" (1 Pet. 1:15-16). This call to be in ethical behavior what we are positionally in Christ captures the essential character of Christian discipleship. A Christian is someone who seeks to consecrate his life more and more to the Lord Jesus Christ. He wants to die to self each and every day, and to be increasingly transformed into Jesus' likeness (cf. 2 Cor. 3:18).

How does this kind of ethical transformation take place in the life of a child of God? It happens progressively over time as the believer applies the teaching of God's word to his attitudes, words, deeds, relationships, and general conduct: "*Sanctify them through thy truth; thy word is truth*" (Jno. 17:17).

This synergistic, or two-sided, work of practical growth in grace—unlike the instantaneous nature of monergistic, eternal sanctification—is gradual and partial. Some of God's children grow more quickly and more maturely than others. Still, *Jehovah-M'Kaddesh* who sanctifies his people and makes them fit for heaven calls them to be saints (cf. 1 Cor. 1:2b) in behavior and practice even now. Whether or not you grow or I develop as we should in this world, what blessed assurance to think that one day both of us shall shine as the sun in the beauty of heavenly holiness, thanks to the amazing grace of *Jehovah-M'Kaddesh*, the Lord who sanctifies his own!

15
Jehovah's Military Names

"The LORD is a man of war; the LORD is his name." (Exodus 15:3)

In this chapter, we will consider two compound names of *Jehovah*: *Jehovah-Sabaoth* and *Jehovah-Nissi*. We group them together because both names suggest military imagery.

Military imagery is pervasive in Scripture because God's people now exist in a world that is under the curse of sin. The present realm is a place of conflict. Only in heaven will we experience perfect harmony and peace. Until the triumphant church is gathered together in one, the militant church is commissioned to fight the good fight of faith.

How thrilling to know, then, that our God is committed to fighting for us and with us in the battles of life! He is the Lord our Banner; He is the Lord of Hosts (or, Armies).

Jehovah-Sabaoth: The Lord of Hosts

Possibly the most pervasive, or frequently used of the compound names of *Jehovah* in Old Testament scripture, is *Jehovah-Sabaoth*, translated by the King James translators by the expression *LORD of hosts*. This name appears at least 270 times in the Old Testament.

The Hebrew word *tsaba*[1], translated "host" speaks of "an army organized for war," or "a great company of soldiers." It first appears in connection with the name of God in Genesis 32:1-2: *"And Jacob went on his way, and the angels of God met him. And when Jacob saw them, he said, This is God's host: and he called the name of that place Mahanaim."* The term is employed to refer to angels, the Hebrew people, insects, and even the New Testament Church.

---

[1] The root of *sabaoth*.

First, in the word of God, ***angels are Jehovah's army***:

- "Bless the LORD, ye his angels, that excel in strength, that do his commandments, hearkening unto the voice of his word. Bless the LORD, all ye his hosts; ye ministers of his, that do his pleasure." (Ps. 103:20-21)

- "...he doeth according to his will in the armies of heaven and among the inhabitants of the earth." (Dan. 4:35b)

- "And suddenly there was with the angel a multitude of the heavenly host praising God, and saying, Glory to God in the highest..." (Lk. 2:13-14a)

- "And the armies which were in heaven followed him upon white horses, clothed in fine linen, white and clean." (Rev. 19:14)

Among the several stories of God dispatching his angelic hosts in battle, the narrative of Elisha and his servant, surrounded by the Syrian army, is especially representative of just what a mighty fighting force are these heavenly warriors:

Therefore [the king of Syria] sent thither horses, and chariots, and a great host: and they came by night, and compassed the city about. And when the servant of the man of God was risen early, and gone forth, behold, an host compassed the city both with horses and chariots. And his servant said unto him, Alas, my master! How shall we do? And he answered, Fear not: for they that be with us are more than they that be with them. And Elisha prayed, and said, LORD, I pray thee, open his eyes, that he may see. And the LORD opened the eyes of the young man; and he saw: and, behold, the mountain was full of horses and chariots of fire round about Elisha. And when they came down to him,

Elisha prayed unto the LORD, and said, Smite this people, I pray
thee, with blindness. And he smote them with blindness
according to the word of Elisha. (2 Kings 6:14-18)

With such a powerful, multitudinous host at our Captain's
command, God's people may find great comfort. *Jehovah-
Sabaoth*, the Lord of heaven's armies, may at any time dispatch
these mighty warriors to do his bidding in defeat of the enemies
of his saints.

Secondly, ***Israel is called Jehovah's host, or army***:

- "But Pharoah shall not hearken unto you, that I may lay my
  hand upon Egypt, and bring forth mine armies, and my people
  the children of Israel, out of the land of Egypt by great
  judgments." (Ex. 7:4)

- "...Wilt not thou, O God, go forth with our hosts? Give us
  help from trouble: for vain is the help of man. Through God
  we shall do valiantly: for he it is that shall tread down our
  enemies." (Ps. 108:11b-13)

- "Again, David gathered together all the chosen men of Israel,
  thirty thousand. And David arose, and went with all the people
  that were with him from Baale of Judah, to bring up from
  thence the ark of God, whose name is called by the name of
  the LORD of hosts [*Jehovah-Sabaoth*] that dwelleth between
  the cherubims... And as soon as David had made an end of
  offering burnt offerings and peace offerings, he blessed the
  people in the name of the LORD of hosts [*Jehovah-Sabaoth*]."
  (2 Sam. 6:1-2, 18)

It is of note that *Jehovah-Sabaoth*, the Lord of hosts, is the
characteristic name for God in 1st and 2nd Samuel. This is

consistent with the militant tone of these narratives surrounding the respective reigns of King Saul and King David.

God can even employ ***insects as his army***. Joel 2:25 is a promise of restoration after judgment: "*And I will restore to you the years that the locust hath eaten, the cankerworm, and the caterpillar, and the palmerworm, my great army which I sent among you.*" These insects had stripped the orchards and fields of fruit and foliage as a Divine judgment upon the disobedient people. God calls them his "great army," doing the bidding of *Jehovah-Sabaoth*.

Finally, ***the Christian Church is compared to an army*** in the New Testament. Military imagery is pervasive in the epistles. Paul, especially, frequently addresses the theme of "spiritual warfare," calling upon his fellow believers to "fight the good fight of faith" and to don the Christian armor (cf. Eph. 6:10ff; 1 Tim. 2:4; 1 Tim. 6:12; 2 Tim. 4:7).

The Messianic prophecy recorded in Isaiah 9:6-7 also forecasts the gospel dispensation in military terms. Notice the reference to *Jehovah-Sabaoth*, the Lord of hosts: "*Of the increase of his government and peace there shall be no end, upon the throne of David, and upon his kingdom, to order it, and to establish it with judgment and with justice from henceforth even for ever. The zeal of the LORD of hosts* [Jehovah-Sabaoth] *will perform this.*"

Even hymnwriters have picked up on this theme. In the familiar hymn, "Onward Christian Soldiers," S. Baring Gould writes,

> *"Like a mighty army moves the church of God;*
> *Brothers, we are treading where the saints have trod..."*

And Martin Luther writes in the battle-hymn of the Protestant Reformation:

> *Did we in our own strength confide,*
> *Our striving would be losing;*

Were not the right Man on our side,
The Man of God's own choosing.
Dost ask who that may be?
Christ Jesus, it is He;
Lord Sabaoth *is His name,*
From age to age the same,
And He must win the battle.

What comfort there is for "soldiers of the cross" to know that *Jehovah-Sabaoth* is their Commander in Chief (cf. Jos. 5:13-15; Is. 6:3, 5). He is "our Shield and Defender" (cf. Gen. 15:1), the Guardian and Protector of his people. Consider the reassurance given to war-weary, beleaguered saints in these passages from the Psalter:

- The LORD of hosts [*Jehovah-Sabaoth*] is with us; the God of Jacob is our refuge. Selah…The LORD of hosts [*Jehovah-Sabaoth*] is with us; the God of Jacob is our refuge. Selah. (Ps. 46:7, 11)

- How amiable are thy tabernacles, O LORD of hosts [*Jehovah-Sabaoth*]! …Yea, the sparrow hath found an house, and the swallow a nest for herself, where she may lay her young, even thine altars, O LORD of hosts [*Jehovah-Sabaoth*], my King, and my God…O LORD God of hosts [*Jehovah-Sabaoth*], hear my prayer: give ear, O God of Jacob. Selah…O LORD of hosts [*Jehovah-Sabaoth*], blessed is the man that trusteth in thee. (Ps. 84:1, 3, 8, 12)

Over and again, Scripture affirms God's promise to fight beside and on behalf of his people:

- Then said David to the Philistine, Thou comest to me with a sword, and with a spear, and with a shield: but I come to thee in the name of the LORD of hosts [*Jehovah-Sabaoth*], the God of the armies of Israel, whom thou hast defied." (1 Sam. 17:45)

- Thou therefore, O LORD God of hosts [*Jehovah-Sabaoth*], the God of Israel, awake to visit all the heathen: be not merciful to any wicked transgressors. Selah. (Ps. 59:5)

- For thus hath the LORD spoken unto me, Like as the lion and the young lion roaring on his prey, when a multitude of shepherds is called forth against him, he will not be afraid of their voice, nor abase himself for the noise of them: so shall the LORD of hosts [*Jehovah-Sabaoth*] come down to fight for mount Zion, and for the hill thereof. As birds flying, so will the LORD of hosts [*Jehovah-Sabaoth*] defend Jerusalem; defending also he will deliver it; and passing over he will preserve it. (Is. 31:4-5)

To every soldier in his army, *Jehovah-Sabaoth* promises his heavenly aid (cf. Ex. 14:14; Deut. 20:3-4; 2 Chr. 20:17; 32:8; Neh. 4:20; Ps. 144:1). It has been said that the military commander flies on the wings of his foot-soldiers. As they march to victory over the enemy, the captain receives the glory for their labors. In the spiritual war against the enemies of righteousness, however, we fly on the wings of the Captain of our salvation. The people of God are victorious because their Captain fights for them.

Nowhere is this more evident than when it comes to the ultimate spiritual war against sin. Singlehandedly, the Lord of hosts fought on behalf of his people at Calvary. As the Second Divine Person prepared to enter the theater of battle in his advent into this world, the prophet depicts him as donning heavenly armor: "*And he saw that there was no man, and wondered that there was no intercessor: therefore his arm brought salvation unto him; and his righteousness, it sustained him. For he put on righteousness as a breastplate, and an helmet of salvation upon his head; and he put on the garments of vengeance for clothing, and was clad with zeal as a cloke"* (Is. 59:16-17).

Also referring to the first coming of Messiah, the prophet Haggai predicts the approaching battle at the cross: *"For thus saith the LORD of hosts* [Jehovah-Sabaoth]; *Yet once, it is a little while, and I will shake the heavens, and the earth, and the sea, and the dry land; and I will shake all nations, and the desire of all nations shall come: and I will fill this house with glory, saith the LORD of hosts* [Jehovah-Sabaoth]" (Hag. 2:6-7).

The Lord Jesus Christ engaged the enemy at the cross and defeated him once and for all: *"But this man, after he had offered one sacrifice for sins for ever, sat down on the right hand of God; from henceforth expecting till his enemies be made his footstool. For by one offering he hath perfected for ever them that are sanctified"* (Heb. 10:12-14). He that is "mighty to save" trod the winepress of the wrath of God alone, "trampling out the vintage" of God's enemies in the greatness of his strength (cf. Is. 63:1-6). Like the clash of Titans, *Jehovah-Sabaoth* met sin, Satan, death, and hell head-on on Golgotha's rugged brow, and vanquished every foe.

Mount Calvary is the ultimate battlefield and the Lord Jesus Christ, the definitive Conqueror. Psalm 24 depicts the victorious Savior's ascension into heaven and coronation at the right hand of the Father. In powerful poetic imagery, the sleeping gates of heaven are ordered to awake and open to receive the returning King:

Lift up your heads, O ye gates; and be ye lift up, ye everlasting doors; and the King of glory shall come in.

Who is this King of glory? The LORD strong and mighty, the LORD mighty in battle.

Lift up your heads, O ye gates; even lift them up, ye everlasting doors; and the King of glory shall come in.

Who is this King of glory? The LORD of hosts [*Jehovah-Sabaoth*], he is the King of glory. Selah. (Ps. 24:7-10)

Jehovah-Nissi: **The Lord our Banner**

The other military image employed as a compound of the name *Jehovah* originates in Exodus 17:15-16: "*And Moses built an altar, and called the name of it Jehovah-nissi: for he said, Because the LORD hath sworn that the LORD will have war with Amalek from generation to generation.*" The name is translated "the Lord our Banner."

The occasion for the revelation of this name was the attack on Israel by the Amalekites in Rephidim. The pilgrim nation was newly delivered from Egyptian bondage, beginning their march toward the land God promised to give them. For the first time, the people encountered an enemy greater than hunger and thirst.

Traveling in the Arabian desert was extremely dangerous at a personal level. Bandits and marauders looked to take advantage of a hapless nomad. A crowd over a million strong like the Israelites would not be alarmed by a few thuggish bandits. A sizeable enemy army, however, like the Amalekites, might score a relatively easy victory against the loosely-organized group of Bedouins. The wandering nomads presented a soft target with the potential for a sizeable booty to the Amalekites.

So Moses commissioned Joshua to assemble a makeshift army to meet the approaching enemy. Meanwhile, Moses, Aaron and Hur assumed an elevated position where they might observe the battle. When the battle ensued, Moses hoisted his staff as he had done over the waters of the Red Sea just weeks previously. When held aloft, the rod of Moses, a visual symbol of God's presence and power, had the effect of a rallying cry to encourage the Hebrew warriors to fight in the name of *Jehovah*. As long as Moses held up his hands, Israel prevailed, but when his hands grew weary and the rod fell from the view of the soldiers, Amalek prevailed. Upon witnessing the relationship between the juxtaposition of the ensign and the progress of the battle, Aaron and Hur assumed positions on either side of Moses, assisting him by upholding his arms, and Joshua and the army won the battle over the enemy (cf. Ex. 17:9-12).

God commanded Moses to include the lesson the nation learned at Rephidim in the oral and written traditions that would be passed down from generation to generation (cf. Ex. 17:14). He intended for this lesson—namely that the people might prevail against their enemies when they maintained perspective on the fact that they fought in the name, for the glory, and under the blessing of *Jehovah* their God—to be remembered. Moses complied by erecting a permanent altar as a memorial to the occasion and naming it *Jehovah-Nissi*, Jehovah is our Banner.

What is the significance of a "banner"? A flag (or standard) is a symbol of identity. Armies have historically carried banners, or flags (cf. S.S. 6:10), and appointed a particular soldier as the standard-bearer to insure that the flag did not fall to the ground. As long as the standard flew, the soldiers knew to fight on. It stood as the army's signal motivating them to rally for the cause. It reminded them who they were and why they were engaged in the current conflict.

Even today, displaying a flag is understood to express allegiance, commitment and devotion to a particular cause. Nations, states and various organizations employ their respective flag designs to distinguish them from others and to unite those within the fraternity under a common cause. Those who identify with the group fly the colors to advertise affinity with that cause.

Do believers in the Lord Jesus Christ share a common cause? Indeed, we do. *Jehovah* is our banner. The glory of God is our cause. The cross of Christ is our standard: *"When the enemy shall come in like a flood, the Spirit of the LORD shall lift up a standard against him. And the Redeemer shall come to Zion, and unto them that turn from transgression in Jacob, saith the LORD"* (Is. 59:19b-20).

"Jesus Christ and him crucified" is the rallying cry of the saints in the gospel day: *"And in that day there shall be a root of Jesse, which shall stand for an ensign of the people; to it shall the Gentiles seek: and his rest shall be glorious"* (Is. 11:10). The great symbol of the church is not a serpent on a pole or a staff held high, but the cross of Jesus Christ: *"And as Moses lifted up the serpent in the wilderness, even so must the Son of man be lifted up: that whosoever believeth in him should not perish, but have eternal life"* (Jno. 3:14-15). Only by a believing gaze upon our crucified and risen Savior, convicted sinners may find the healing of assurance and relief from the burden of sin, like Bunyan's pilgrim found relief when he saw the cross and like bitten Israelites found healing when they saw the brazen serpent (cf. Is. 45:22).

Have you seen the cross? Only as this standard is raised aloft in the gospel so Christian soldiers may see it will they prevail in the spiritual war they fight with the devil. May every gospel preacher, then, lift it high and display it clearly so that all may see it:

Thou hast given a banner to them that fear thee, that it may be displayed because of the truth. (Ps. 60:4)

We will rejoice in thy salvation, and in the name of our God we will set up our banners... (Ps. 20:5).

PART 4

THE CHRISTIAN NAMES

16
Jesus: Jehovah is Salvation

"And thou shalt call his name Jesus, for he shall save his people from their sins."
(Matthew 1:21)

A s we have seen, each of the Divine names reveals a feature
of God's character. One name, however, includes and
encapsulate all the rest. It is the name above every other name
(cf. Phi. 2:12)—the precious name of *Jesus*.

Jesus means "Jehovah is Salvation." It is the name that
expresses God's nature in comprehensive terms, for Jesus is
"God manifest in the flesh" (1 Tim. 3:16). In Jesus, the fullness of
the Godhead dwelt bodily (Col. 1:19; 2:9). He is *"the express
image of God's person"* (Heb. 1:3), the complete expression of
who God is (Jno. 1:18), the *Alpha and Omega* (i.e. the complete
alphabet) and *the Word* of God (Rev. 1:8; Jno. 1:1-2, 14). To see
Jesus is to see God (Jno. 14:9), for Jesus *"manifested* [i.e.
revealed] *the Father's name to the men God gave Him out of the
world"* (Jno. 17:6)

The name *Jesus* is the Greek form of *Joshua* or *Jehoshua*. It
was a name given from heaven, for the child born to Mary would
indeed *"save His people from their sins"* (Mt. 1:21). It is a
wonderful name—a name of great honor. Though it was a
common name among Jewish people in the Old Testament,
history indicates that Jewish people stopped using it after about
the second century A.D.

This "name above every name"—a name that expresses both
his Divine authority and redemptive purpose—calls for a
response of humble obedience from men (Phi. 2:9-10). It is the
*"only name under heaven given among men whereby we must be
saved"* (Acts 4:12), for he alone is mighty to save. It is a name of
inestimable power, for it expresses everything that God is –
"...His name, through faith in His name, hath made this man

strong..." (Acts 3:6,16). It is a name so precious that saints esteem it an honor to suffer for it (Acts 5:31). It is a *"worthy name,"* assumed by those who have professed faith in him (Jas. 2:7; 2 Tim. 2:19), and the honor and glory of which is their ultimate priority: *"That the name of our Lord Jesus Christ may be glorified in you, and ye in Him, according to the grace of our God and the Lord Jesus Christ"* (2 Ths. 1:12).

Consider the many ways in which the name *Jesus* contains and embraces every Old Testament name of God. John 1:1-14, Colossians 1:16-17, Hebrews 1:2 and 1 Peter 4:19 indicate that *Jesus* is *Elohim*, the faithful Creator. John 8:56 and Hebrews 13:8 affirm that *Jesus* is the eternally present, preexistent "I AM," and Hebrews 9:12 and 1 Peter 1:18 that he is the Redeemer, both of which truths are revealed in the name *Jehovah*. And John 13:13-14, as well as John 20:28, show that he is the authoritative *Adonai*, our Lord and Master.

What about the compound names in relation to both *Elohim* and *Jehovah*? This chart indicates that Jesus fulfills and embodies every detail of each Divine name.

Name	Significance	Parallel
El-Shaddai	Bountiful, All-Sufficient	Eph. 3:20; Heb. 7:25; Phi. 4:19; Jude 24
El-Elyon	Supremacy/Sovereignty	Mt. 28:18; Eph. 1:20-21; Rev. 19:16
El-Olam	Eternal Character/Purpose	Eph. 3:10-11; Eph. 2:7; 1 Tim. 6:15
Jehovah-Jireh	Providence	Jno. 1:29; 1 Pet. 1:18
Jehovah-Rophe	Health-giving	Mt. 8:17; Lk. 4:18; Rev. 21:7
Jehovah-Shalom	Reconciliation	2 Cor. 5:18-20; Eph. 2:14
Jehovah-Tsidkenu	Justification	1 Cor. 1:30; 2 Cor. 5:21
Jehovah-M'Kaddesh	Sanctification	1 Cor. 1:30; Heb. 10:10; 13:12
Jehovah-Sabaoth	Spiritual Warfare	Is. 59:16-18; Ps. 24:10

There is saving power in the name, i.e. in the person or character represented by the name, of Jesus: *"Neither is there salvation in any other, for there is no other name under heaven given among men whereby we must be saved"* (Acts 4:12). Why is Jesus, meaning *Jehovah is salvation*, the only Savior? Jesus alone can save sinners because he is *Jehovah* incarnate: "*I, even I*

only, am the LORD [Jehovah], *and beside me, there is no savior"*
(Is. 43:11). Some of the members of the Corinthian Church were
outstanding testimonials to the saving power of the Lord Jesus,
simply by virtue of the kinds of immorality from which they had
been delivered: *"And such were some of you, but ye are washed,
but ye are justified, but ye are sanctified, in the name of the Lord
Jesus and by the Spirit of our God"* (1 Cor. 6:11).

There is saving help in the name of Jesus not only so far as
eternal salvation is concerned, but also in terms of the many
kinds of deliverance God's child needs as he passes through this
world. The familiar Christian hymn powerfully captures this
thought:

> *Take the name of Jesus with you*
> *Child of sorrow, and of woe;*
> *It will joy and comfort give you;*
> *Take it, then, where'er you go.*

> *Take the name of Jesus ever*
> *As a shield from every snare;*
> *If temptations round you gather,*
> *Breathe that holy name in prayer.*

In the timeless Christian hymn (and my personal favorite)
"How Sweet the Name of Jesus Sounds," 17th century English
pastor John Newton takes his cue from Song of Solomon 1:3:
*"Because of the savor of thy good ointments thy name is as
ointment poured forth; therefore do the virgins love thee."* From
this metaphorical springboard, Newton begins:

> *How sweet the name of Jesus sounds*
> *In a believer's ear;*

This descriptive comparison between the name of *Jesus* and a
sweet perfume[1] suggests a benefit that is not simply an object of

practical value, but one that delights the senses, like the pleasant aroma of a rose garden or honeysuckle orchard. Just as the Shulamite compares the hearing of Solomon's name to the sensory delights generated by a luxurious perfume, so Newton finds a sweet fragrance in the mere mention of the name of *Jesus*. Beside this initial image of an aromatic perfume, consider the many other metaphors he employs to describe the preciousness of *Jesus'* name:

First, the name of *Jesus* is ***a spiritual balm and medicine***, soothing, healing and calming:

> *It soothes his sorrows, heals his wounds,*
> *And drives away his fears.*
> *It makes the wounded spirit whole*
> *And calms the troubled breast;*

Secondly, the name of *Jesus* is ***manna*** to feed and revive the hungry soul—

> *'Tis manna to the hungry soul,*

And ***a soft pillow*** on which the faint may find repose—

> *And to the weary, rest.*

Next, Newton compares *Jesus'* name to ***a solid foundation*** on which to construct a life...

> *Dear name, the Rock on which I build...*

...A ***safe refuge*** in the storm and protection from danger...

> *My shield and hiding place...*

---

[1] *Savor* means "fragrance." *Ointment* suggests the thought of a "perfume."

...And *a bank* with inexhaustible capital resources:

> *My never failing treasury filled*
> *With boundless stores of grace.*

Finally, he employs the image of *a beautiful melody* to describe the delight found in the name of *Jesus*:

> *And may the music of thy name*
> *Refresh my soul in death.*

There are over 700 names and titles ascribed to the Lord Jesus Christ in the Bible, and every name he wears is a blessing that he shares. Newton includes a few of these precious names in verse four of his hymn:

> *Jesus, my Shepherd, Husband, Friend*
> *My Prophet, Priest, and King;*
> *My Lord, my Life, my Way, my End,*
> *Accept the praise I bring*

Have you discovered the music intrinsic to the name of *Jesus*? Do you think of him as your Redeemer, your Shepherd, your King, or the Friend of sinners? How often do you reflect on Jesus as the great I AM? Have you ever discovered him to be your Light in this dark world, the Bread that satisfies the hunger in your heart, the Living Water that quenches the thirst of your parched soul?

The revelation of the name of *Jesus* is the pinnacle of God's self-disclosure to men. Every other name—*El-Shaddai, El-Elyon, Jehovah-Jireh, Jehovah-Rophe, Jehovah-Tsidkenu,* and all the rest—are distilled and comprehended in this name above every other name. He is *Jehovah our Savior*, who came for the express purpose of saving his people from their sins. And he lived up to the name, i.e. he secured salvation on behalf of all who were given to him by the Father before the world began.

Jesus is not merely a potential Savior, or a hypothetical Savior. He did not come into this world merely to make salvation possible if man will cooperate with it or accept the offer of it. He came to make salvation a reality—to secure it on behalf of God's elect. There are no "ifs" in Matthew 1:21. The angel's good news was *"He shall save his people,"* not "He shall save if the sinner will let him." Our good news as gospel preachers today is "He came to save, and he did it." Therefore, those for whom Jesus died are saved, with nothing further to be added to make it a fact.

If any for whom Jesus died on the cross are sent to hell, then, it follows that "saved" people will be in hell. Since no principle of Scripture or logic would support such a preposterous conclusion, then we must affirm that everyone on whose behalf the Lord Jesus suffered and died will see his face in heavenly bliss. Thinking people realize at this point in the argument that if everyone for whom Jesus' died is actually saved and will never be sent to hell, then, the simple law of non-contradiction requires the affirmation that Jesus did not die for every human being. In a word, the scope and extent of the atonement is definite and particular, not general and unlimited, else Jesus did not live up to his name as "Savior."

Those who feel themselves to be unworthy sinners do indeed find music, then, in the name of *Jesus*. It is a soft pillow on which to rest their weary, sin-sick souls. This precious name is a sweet fragrance, a healing balm, a refuge from danger, a solid foundation on which to construct both a faith and a life that will stand the tests of time.

My good friend and fellow minister, Elder Ralph Harris, captures the preciousness of this most sublime of names in his hymn-poem *Jesus, Blessed Jesus*.[2] It will make for a fitting conclusion to this chapter:

---

[2] *Old School Hymnal, Eleventh Edition*, #513. Copyright © 1983 by Old School Hymnal Co., Inc. Used by permission.

My dear Jesus, blessed Jesus;
What a grand and gracious theme!
Oh, the precious name of Jesus;
What a bright and brilliant beam!
Oh, my Jesus, dearest Jesus;
How I love to hear the sound!
Thou whose name is filled with music,
May I in Thy love be found.

Precious Jesus, fairest Jesus;
May I love Thee as I should.
Thou art altogether lovely;
Thou art altogether good.
Oh, sweet Jesus, wondrous Jesus;
What great works Thy hands have wrought!
What great things for wretched sinners!
Oh, how precious is the thought!

Oh, Thou gracious loving Jesus!
Would'st Thou raise me to Thy feet?
So that in such hallowed posture,
Thy dear name I might repeat.
Jesus, Jesus, lovely Jesus,
I would dwell before Thy throne;
Praying, praising, seeking, finding;
Ever humbly pressing on.

Oh dear Jesus! My Lord Jesus,
How I love to speak Thy name!
Thou art lovely on our mountains,
In our valleys You're the same.
Precious Jesus, my dear Savior;
Thou Thy Father's darling Son;
How we hope one day to see Thee!

When our race down here is run.

Does the romantic tone of this Christian hymn-poem, or of the Divinely inspired book known as *Solomon's Song*, make you uncomfortable? It shouldn't. In fact, it expresses genuine Christian experience—an experience that is not merely academic or practical, but aesthetic and affective. Authentic Christianity, in other words, is not merely concerned with the true and the good, but also with the beautiful; not only the head and the hands, but also the heart.

It bears repeating that Christian discipleship is not a business contract with God. Neither is it merely a mutually beneficial hierarchy, e. g. employer/employee or teacher/student relationship, in which one assumes a role of subjection to another for some symbiotic end. Christianity is essentially a love relationship with the Lord Jesus Christ, like a husband/wife dynamic. We neglect this romantic dimension of Christianity at our peril. So, regardless of individual temperament, the sensible sinner will find a melody in the name of *Jesus* that speaks to the depths of spiritual need in his heart. If you have been brought to see your own need of this Savior, then reflect often on this most blessed Person, and take the name of *Jesus* with you, everywhere you go.

17
Abba: **God our Father**

"And because ye are sons, God hath sent forth the Spirit of his Son into your hearts, crying, Abba, Father." (Galatians 4:6)

T he last, and most sublime name for God revealed in Holy Scripture is the intimate title *Abba*, meaning "Father." As surprising and potentially irreverent it may sound to a Jewish person, "Father" is how the believer in Jesus Christ is taught to address God. The reputable Christian theologian and author, J. I. Packer, makes the point clearly:

> You sum up the whole of New Testament religion if you describe it as the knowledge of God as one's holy Father. If you want to judge how well a person understands Christianity, find out how much he makes of the thought of being God's child, and having God as his Father. If this is not the thought that prompts and controls his worship and prayers and his whole outlook on life, it means that he does not understand Christianity very well at all.
>
> For everything that Christ taught, everything that makes the New Testament new, and better than the Old, everything that is distinctively Christian as opposed to merely Jewish, is summed up in the knowledge of the Fatherhood of God. 'Father' is the Christian name for God. Our understanding of Christianity cannot be better than our grasp of adoption.[1]

It was the protestant theologian Karl Barth (1886-1968) who first referenced the Trinitarian formula for baptism in Matthew 28:19—the instruction to the apostles to administer baptism to believers *"in the name[2] of the Father, and of the Son, and of the*

---

[1] J.I. Packer, *Knowing God*, pp. 201-202.

Holy Spirit"—in terms of "the Christian name for God." But Andrew Jukes agrees:

> Just in proportion as we really know that God is 'Father, Son, and Holy Ghost,' we shall reflect something of the fellowship and love, which such a name declares to us.[3]

This Trinitarian name for God is daringly revolutionary. When the Lord Jesus in his first sermon taught his disciples to pray saying, "*Our Father, which art in heaven...*", he espoused an idea so innovative that it bordered on sacrilege, at least in the perception of the Jewish religious leaders.

Father, Son and Holy Ghost is a filial[4] name—a name suggesting an intimacy of relationship within the Godhead. It defines the relationship that exists between the three Divine Persons in terms of a father/son dynamic. When Jesus in prayer addressed himself to God as "*Father*" (Jno. 17:5, 21, 24), "*Holy Father*" (Jno. 17:11), and "*Righteous Father*" (Jno. 17:25), he expresses a kind of intimacy with God that the Rabbis would have considered "out of bounds."

This name is daring and revolutionary, then, because it is so personal. There is no record in Jewish literature of anyone ever addressing God in such a personal way. For instance, a typical Jewish prayer (or *tefillah*) offered three times daily says, "*Blessed art thou, Yahweh, God of Abraham, God of Isaac, God of Jacob, the most High God, Master of heaven and earth, our Shield and the Shield of our fathers; blessed art thou, Yahweh, the Shield of Abraham.*"   Indeed, God had revealed himself to Israel in personal, loving and familial terms (cf. Ex. 4:22; Deut. 32:6; Jer. 31:9; Hos. 11:1; Mal. 1:6), but no Jewish person would dare refer to him as "Father" for fear of presuming upon the holiness of

---

[2] Notice that "name" is singular.
[3] Andrew Jukes, *The Names of God*, p. 178.
[4] *Filial* means "relating to a family; assuming the relation of a child, or offspring."

God. Jesus teaches, however, that such a reference is not an expression of presumption, but of faith.

Christians call God "Father" for three reasons. First, *Jesus himself taught us to think of God, and to invoke him in prayer, by this title* (cf. Mt. 6:9). That early Christians began to practice this intimate form of address in their prayers is evident by Peter's description of a praying believer in terms of a person who "calls on the Father": "*And if ye call on the Father, who without respect of persons judgeth according to every man's work, pass the time of your sojourning here in fear*" (1 Pet. 1:17).

Secondly, we call God "Father" because of *the doctrine of spiritual union*. The Lord Jesus taught His disciples that his Father is also their Father (cf. Jno. 20:17; Mt. 6:26). Because he is "the God and Father of Christ" and because Christ is "our Lord," he is also our Father (Eph. 1:3). In other words, believers may call God "Father" only by virtue of their spiritual union with Jesus Christ (Jno. 14:6b). Sonship is a blessing that is ours through his only begotten Son, the Lord Jesus Christ (Rom. 8:29).

It has been suggested by some that the Model Prayer recorded in Matthew 6:9-13 is not a Christian prayer at all because there is no mention of praying "in Jesus' name." I offer for your consideration, however, that the very fact that the disciples of Jesus are encouraged to approach God as "Father" assumes that they come before him by virtue of the merits of Christ, for apart from his sacrificial death on their behalf, no relationship with God as "Father" would exist.

Thirdly, we call God "Father" because *the Holy Spirit creates this Divine impulse in the soul* (Gal. 4:6). He adopts us into God's family and witnesses in our hearts to the reality of Divine sonship (Rom. 8:14-16). *Abba* is Aramaic for "father"—probably one of the first sounds a baby learned to make. It is not only appropriate but natural for those whose hearts have been tendered by God's Spirit to speak freely and personally to God, just like any little child would to his father. *Pater* is Greek for "father."

Thus by uniting the Aramaic term with the Greek, Paul teaches that both Jews and Gentiles can call God "Father" through the Lord Jesus Christ.

What does this sublime name for God imply? The Fatherhood of God involves several thrilling, existential blessings for us. First, *Father* implies **love**. Because he is our Father, we, his children, are dearly loved (cf. Jno. 16:27; 1 Jno. 3:1). It also implies **compassion**: "*Like as a father pitieth his children, so the LORD pitieth them that fear him. For he knoweth our frame; he remembereth that we are dust*" (Ps. 103:13-14; cf. 2 Cor. 1:3).

In the third place, Divine Fatherhood implies **belonging**. Because he is our Father, we belong to a family and heaven is our home (cf. Jno. 14:2). Likewise, it implies **grace**. Because God is our Father, he rejoices to welcome home his repentant child (cf. Lk. 15:11-24). Fifthly, it includes the idea of **education**. Because God is our Father, he is committed to teaching and training his children (cf. Hos. 11:2; Heb. 12:5-11).

In the sixth place, the Fatherhood of God involves the idea of **provision**. Because he is our Father, God knows and promises to provide for the needs of his children (cf. Lk. 11:11, 13; 12:30). Further, it implies **identity**. With God as our Father, we, his children, bear the family name (cf. Eph. 3:14). Finally, *Father* implies **freedom**. Because he is our heavenly Father, we may draw nigh to him in prayer, speaking freely and confidently to him without fear of rejection or reprisal (cf. Heb. 4:16).

What amazing kind of love has been bestowed upon us that we might be called the children of God! This incalculable blessing of sonship in God's family prompted Charles Wesley to write:

> *Oh, how should I the goodness tell,*
> *Father which Thou to me hast showed,*
> *That I, a child of wrath and hell,*
> *I should be called a child of God;*

> *Should know, should feel my sins forgiven,*

Blest with this antepast of heaven!

This is exactly the kind of existential effect the knowledge of God as our Father should have on us, his children. May God help me to never take such a privilege for granted. May I never permit the familiarity intrinsic to this intimate relationship with God to breed an attitude of complacency or entitlement in my heart, for this precious name *Abba* and the privilege of calling on God by this name by means of the Lord Jesus Christ is truly life eternal (cf. Jno. 17:3).

www.ingramcontent.com/pod-product-compliance
Lightning Source LLC
Chambersburg PA
CBHW032057080426

42733CB00006B/308